中英譯學協會

Computers, Language Reform, and Lexicography in China

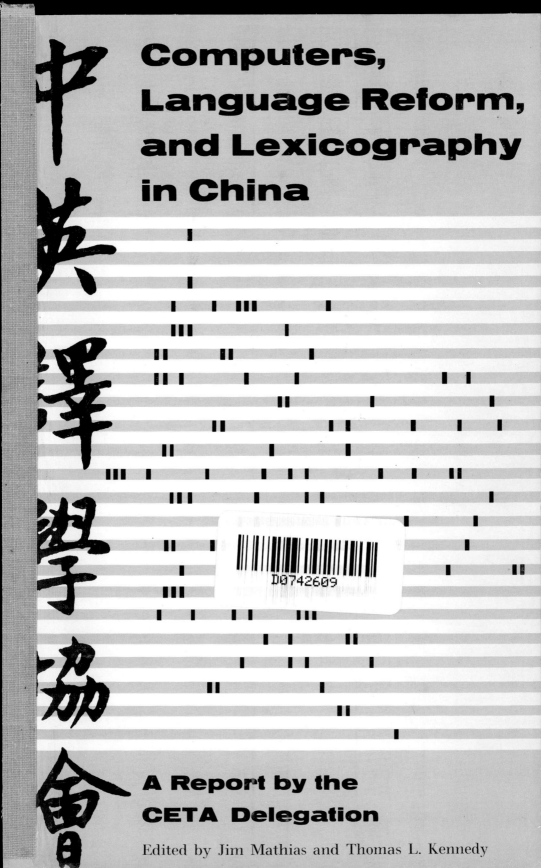

D0742609

A Report by the CETA Delegation

Edited by Jim Mathias and Thomas L. Kennedy

Computers, Language Reform, and Lexicography in China

A Report by the CETA Delegation

Edited by Jim Mathias and Thomas L. Kennedy

OTHER DELEGATION MEMBERS

Irving Antin
Kieran Broadbent
Thomas Coffey
Thomas Creamer
Robert Dunn

Vivian Hsu
Martin Kay
Henry Louie
James McHale
T. C. Ting

Washington State University Press

Printed in the United States of America
ISBN-0-87422-0157

ACKNOWLEDGMENTS

This report was made possible through the work of members of the Delegation and the combined support of many organizations.

The Chinese-English Translation Assistance (CETA) Group sponsored the CETA Delegation trip, and provided the planning, organization, and management services.

The National Endowment for the Humanities gave significant assistance through a research grant which covered a major portion of the travel costs.

The Xerox Palo Alto Research Center provided facilities for computer production of interim draft versions of the report.

Finally, special recognition is due to CETA staff members, particularly Nina Halm, for the careful proofing without which the editors' task would have been much more difficult.

*　　*　　*

The findings and conclusions presented here do not necessarily represent the views of the supporting organizations.

*　　*　　*

This report includes the shared experiences of all members of the Delegation. The editors are responsible for selection and organization of the information and for the style of presentation.

CETA

关于中英译学协会的说明

中英译学协会是由四十所大学和美国政府各机关的语言学家翻译员,学者和电子计算机专家所组成的.它是一个具有独立性和国际性的组织.此组织创始于一九七一年.它利用电子计算技术来汇编汉英词典及探究如何在翻译工作上应用电子计算机.本协会的词典编辑工作以及主要方针制定委员会的委员均由各方人士以义务身份参加.协会书记处有四人管理协会的日常工作.本协会使用的电子计算机与管理人员开支费用的由政府各部门和私人基金会提供.

中英译学协会的主要出版物包括一本十一万条活叶汉英词典的原稿,一套五十万条科学技术汉英初稿的缩微胶片,一本一千条的现代汉英俗语词典即将由耶鲁大学远东印刷公司出版,以及一本已经校对即将出版的汉语词典目录.本协会所有词典与汉语词典目录完全是用电子计算机来存储,校订和打印.

本协会经常与有关词典编辑人士交换资料及考究电子计算机对语言学与机器翻译的作用.此外本协会并召集和参加各种有关会议以及发表技术性的文章和中英译学协会简报以促进国际上有关编辑汉语词典资料的交流.

CETA

P.O. Box 400
9811 Connecticut Avenue
Kensington, Maryland 20795

The CETA (Chinese-English Translation Assistance) Group is an independent international organization of linguists, translators, scholars, and computer specialists from many government offices and over forty academic institutions. It was founded in 1971 to compile Chinese-English dictionaries utilizing computer technology and to explore application of computers in translation. The lexicographic and editorial services used by CETA are provided by participants on a voluntary basis, and membership on the committees which establish the major policies is also voluntary. CETA's day-to-day work is conducted by a secretariat staff of four persons which is responsible for the management of CETA projects. The computer services and operating funds for the staff are contributed by a number of different government departments and private foundations.

The main products of CETA's efforts have been (1) a draft of a general Chinese-English dictionary of 110,000 terms in loose-leaf form; (2) a preliminary Chinese-English dictionary of 500,000 scientific and technical terms issued in microfiche; (3) an 11,000-term *Modern Chinese Colloquial Dictionary* about to be printed by Far Eastern Publications, Yale University; and (4) a revised *Bibliography of 2,000 Chinese Dictionaries*, also near publication. All of the CETA dictionaries and the bibliography are stored, revised, and printed using computers.

Through daily business contact, the CETA organization maintains a constant exchange of information about Chinese dictionaries, applications of computers to linguistics, and machine translation. In addition, CETA arranges and participates in conferences, prepares technical papers, and distributes the *CETA Bulletin* to foster an international exchange of information on these topics.

Contents

1 Introduction

CETA DELEGATION TO CHINA

In April, 1979, the CETA (Chinese-English Translation Assistance) Language, Lexicography, and Computer Applications Delegation visited the People's Republic of China. Led by Jim Mathias of CETA and Thomas Kennedy of Washington State University, the delegation consisted of Irving Antin, Southern Illinois University; Kieran Broadbent, International Development Research Centre, Ottawa; Thomas Coffey, freelance translator; Thomas Creamer, CETA; Robert Dunn, Library of Congress; Vivian Hsu, Oberlin College; Martin Kay, Xerox Palo Alto Research Center; Henry Louie, Foreign Broadcast Information Service; James McHale, Voice of America; and T. C. Ting, National Bureau of Standards. Sixteen full- or half-day meetings were held with over one hundred Chinese lexicographers, linguists, teachers, librarians, and computer specialists from the following institutions: Institute of Scientific and Technical Information of China (ISTIC); Beijing Foreign Languages Institute; Institute of Linguistics and Philology, Chinese Academy of Social Sciences (Beijing); Committee for Reforming the Chinese Written Language (Beijing); Institute of Computing Technology, Chinese Academy of Sciences (Beijing); Beijing National Library; State Publications Bureau (Beijing); Commercial Press (Beijing); Nanjing University; Shanghai Foreign Languages Institute; Fudan University (Shanghai); Shanghai Normal University; Shanghai Computer Factory; Jiaotong University (Shanghai); Shanghai Language Society; Shanghai Institute of Automation; Editing Group of *A Large English-Chinese Dictionary*.

We were pleasantly surprised with the warm reception we received at all institutions and at the considerable effort expended by our Chinese hosts to adjust their schedules and itinerary whenever we asked for changes. The Chinese teachers, researchers, and administrators we met were more open in their communication with Western counterparts than had been reported by previous American delegations.

The principal areas discussed with Chinese specialists were lexicography, language reform, computer applications, and information services. The Chinese have made great progress in lexicography as is evident from their published dictionaries, revision of a new edition (1979) *Cihai,* and work in progress on traditional and modern-language dictionaries. We inquired about the status of language reform everywhere we went. It seemed that there is some retrenchment. The Chinese no longer expect to achieve the widespread use of *pinyin* in the immediate future, and implementation of the Second Draft Plan for Simplified Characters has been delayed for further study. However, they are actively promoting the use of *putonghua,* and there was no evidence of a change in the overall direction of language reform. The specialists at Beijing National Library and Nanjing University Library were interested in exchanging information about library automation with libraries in other countries. Though both libraries expressed the desire to continue receiving Library of Congress machine readable cataloging (MARC) documentation, tapes, and manuals, the application of computer processing to library work is still in the experimental or planning stages. It was evident that the Chinese in all universities and institutions visited attach importance to computer development, especially Chinese character-input methods. Some modern techniques such as thin film memory have been incorporated in the computers used for research. Also, some research is being done for on-line input. However, there is little interactive environment, and there is little evidence of miniaturization. In general, the Chinese we met appear to understand new technology concepts but lack the resources to implement features requiring extensive production and quality-control capabilities.

As for the person in the street, many appear to be trying to learn foreign languages. This characteristic was frequently noticed in the hotel employees, guides, cart pullers, store clerks, students, and children who approached individual members of the CETA group for assistance in correcting pronunciation, English idiom, or grammar. Two of the delegation (while walking in the evening on the streets of Guilin) were asked by two teacher-training students to record a few pages of English-language text. The voice recordings were to be used for "correcting pronunciation." Such incidents were not unusual. If modernization is the key, then foreign languages and access to foreign-language scientific and technological materials become critical elements in improving one's position.

The willingness to exchange information and services with the CETA group is an indication of Chinese interest in cooperation with scholars in the United States. We expect that as long as the present political climate continues there will be further exchanges of reports, computer data, services, and visits between CETA and Chinese counterparts.

2 Lexicography

The CETA Delegation reviewed the latest developments in Chinese lexicography in meetings with the Linguistic Institute of the Chinese Academy of Sciences, Beijing Foreign Languages Institute, Nanjing University, Fudan University, and the Shanghai Foreign Languages Institute. We obtained additional information, especially related to scientific and technical dictionaries, by surveying the main bookstores in Beijing, Nanjing, and Shanghai.

Characteristically, each dictionary group with which we met criticized its work as being inadequate. Although we have not yet systematically studied the more than forty dictionaries purchased on the trip, we were quite impressed with the level of scholarship demonstrated. However, in view of the constant references by Chinese lexicographers to the importance of up-to-date terminology, it is interesting to note that they have not yet compiled a dictionary of political terms and slogans. Lexicographers at Fudan University expressed a strong interest in preparing such a dictionary, and now that the political uncertainties from the Cultural Revolution and the post-Mao succession appear to be mollified, a dictionary of political expressions may soon be available.

This section is divided into the following four parts: general language dictionaries, classical or premodern dictionaries, current dictionary projects, and scientific and technical dictionaries.

GENERAL LANGUAGE DICTIONARIES

Although the publication of classical and scientific and technical dictionaries is being stressed in China, no lexical effort is assigned more importance than the production of general language dictionaries. As noted elsewhere in this report, there is something of a foreign-language demand underway in China. To meet this popular demand and, more importantly, to produce more adequate reference tools for the growing corps of translators, lexicographers in China are compiling dictionaries at an unprecedented pace. The main organizations involved in dictionary projects are the Linguistics Institute of the Chinese Academy of Sciences and the Foreign Languages Institutes in Beijing and Shanghai. In Guangzhou, however, we purchased a copy of the *Hanyu Chengyu Cidian*, an excellent idiom dictionary compiled at Gansu Normal University, which shows the geographical dispersion of dictionary building in China.

XIANDAI HANYU CIDIAN 现代汉语词典

In 1978, after twenty years of work, the Commercial Press published the *Xiandai Hanyu Cidian (Modern Chinese Dictionary)* by the Chinese Academy of Sciences. It represents the most important dictionary produced in China since the publication of the *Guoyu Cidian*. Because it is taken as the authoritative reference for the latest dictionary efforts such as the Beijing Foreign Languages Institute's *Chinese-English Dictionary* and the Shanghai Foreign Languages Institute's *Han-E Cidian*, it merits close study. A 1977 draft edition of the dictionary was reprinted in Hong Kong and Japan and is widely available in the West. The 1978 *Xiandai* has been revised and contains three thousand more entries than the old edition. Simplified characters are used in listing all combinations, which was not the case with the 1977 edition. Curiously, the editors of the revised version removed all scientific and technical labels.

The *Xiandai* includes approximately twelve thousand single characters and fifty-six thousand entries. Single characters are arranged by *pinyin* and tone, but the sequence within each *pinyin* section is, as yet, undetermined. Characters are printed in simplified form with the traditional form listed in parentheses alongside. If only the radical element of a character has been simplied, such as 讠 in 说 , or 贝 in 质 , or 纟 in 给 , the traditional form is not given. If a character has distinct meanings, each meaning is listed as a separate entry. For example, the character 封 *(feng)* appears twice as a lead character. The first time it is defined as "to confer a title and land to a member of the nobility" and as a surname. The second entry defines it as "to seal off," "to close," "a measure word for letter," and so forth.

Combinations are arranged by *pinyin* and tone under each lead character. Definitions are clearly written, well annotated, and labelled where necessary. The main linguistic classifiers are 方 for regional, 口 for colloquial, 书 for literary, and 囧 for rare. Figurative or metaphorical meanings are indicated by a 囗 . The symbol // indicates that the combination can be separated and other components inserted between the characters or that it can act as a suffix. The dictionary also extensively cross-references variant pronunciations and alternate meanings. Finally, if a combination is a transliteration of a foreign word, the source language and original spelling are given.

The *Xiandai* includes *pinyin*, radical, and four-corner indices; a chronology of Chinese history; a list of weights and measures; the scheme for the Chinese phonetic alphabet; a periodic chart;

and a list of the most common names for some of the components (偏旁) of Chinese characters.

A CHINESE-ENGLISH DICTIONARY 汉英词典

In 1971 the sixty-man dictionary group of the English Department at the Beijing Foreign Languages Institute, under the direction of Professor Wu Jingrong, began compiling *A Chinese-English Dictionary*. The dictionary was published in China at the end of 1978 and immediately sold out. A second printing is now available from Hong Kong and Japan.

The *Chinese-English Dictionary* was compiled as a research tool for junior translators at the Institute. In the opinion of Professor Wu's dictionary group, all contemporary Chinese-English dictionaries were outdated, and a new dictionary was needed. Toward this end a special effort was made to record the modern Chinese language and collect political, scientific, and colloquial terms in general use. Archaic, rare, and obsolete terms are included, but only those one might encounter in reading modern literature.

Work on the dictionary was divided among three groups. One surveyed the *Xiandai Hanyu Cidian, Cihai, Ciyuan, Guoyu Cidian*, and the *Xinhua Zidian* for entries of a general nature. A second group collected scientific and technical terms. After provisional definitions were written, the drafts were sent to the appropriate agencies of the Academy of Sciences for review. On occasion the editors visited factories and communes to obtain information and criticism regarding technical terminology. The third group gathered terms from the social sciences by reading primary sources such as newspapers, magazines, and contemporary books. In all, the dictionary contains more than six thousand single characters and fifty-seven thousand combinations.

The dictionary is arranged by *pinyin* and tone according to standards established by the *Xinhua Zidian*. Within each *pinyin* section, single characters are listed by total strokes. If a character has alternate pronunciations, they are treated as individual entries and listed separately under the appropriate *pinyin* heading. All characters are given in their simplified form only (a conversion chart of simplified to traditional characters is included as an appendix). Each lead character is clearly defined, with examples illustrating different syntactical functions.

Character combinations are listed under each lead character in *pinyin* order. Where applicable, each entry is identified by discipline, such as medicine, metallurgy, military, and so forth. As with the lead characters, the definitions of character combinations are supplemented by illustrative examples. This approach may be contrasted with that of other recent Chinese-English dictionaries such as the

Han Ying Xiao Cidian (*A Small Chinese-English Dictionary*, Beijing, 1976; reprinted in Hong Kong as *A Current Chinese-English Dictionary*, 1978) and the *Xiuzhen Hanying Cidian* (*A Pocket Chinese-English Dictionary*, Beijing, 1976), which indicate parts of speech. The editors of the *Chinese-English Dictionary* felt that contextual examples to indicate usage would be more effective and more in keeping with the nature of the Chinese language.

A radical index and a *pinyin* index are at the front of the *Chinese-English Dictionary*. It should be noted that the dictionary uses 227 radicals (rather than the traditional 214) and that the sequence of the radicals differs slightly from the arrangement familiar to most Western students. In the back of the dictionary are the following: the original complex forms of 352 Chinese characters and their simplified versions; the scheme for the Chinese phonetic alphabet; the Chinese phonetic alphabet and Wade-Giles systems; consonants and vowels of the Chinese phonetic alphabet and their corresponding international phonetic symbols; countries, regions, capitals, and currencies; a brief Chinese chronology; a table of chemical elements; units of weights and measures; the "Heavenly Stems and Earthy Branches"; and the twenty-four solar terms.

A CHINESE-RUSSIAN DICTIONARY 汉俄词典

The *Han-E Cidian* (*Chinese-Russian Dictionary*) was compiled at the Shanghai Foreign Languages Institute. Intended for use by college students and in general translation work, the dictionary concentrates on the modern Chinese language, although some literary terms of older vintage are included. The editors collected 400,000-500,000 entries and examples on index cards by reading contemporary books and periodicals. They also consulted other dictionaries, especially for scientific and technical terms. Draft manuscripts were issued in 1965, 1966, and 1972. The final edition was published in 1977 and includes over five thousand single characters and fifty thousand combinations.

Both lead characters and character combinations in the *Chinese-Russian Dictionary* are arranged according to *pinyin* and tone. Lead-character definitions are divided into subgroups whenever discrete meanings exist. For example, the definition for the character *mao* 毛 is divided into three sections. The first section gives the meanings "hair," "feathers," etc; the second section gives meanings for "fear," "panic," and so forth; while the third section indicates that the character is a colloquial variant of *jiao* 角 (*renminbi* denomination). This format is identical to that of the *Xiandai Hanyu Cidian*, but differs from that of the Beijing Foreign Languages Institute's *Chinese-English Dictionary*, which combines all the information in a paragraph.

Character combinations are listed in *pinyin* order underneath the lead character. Many of these definitions are augmented by the inclusion of illustrative phrases or sentences. The compilers also use labels and symbols to: specify disciplines (seventy-two) within symbols < >; separate examples from definitions by the symbol | |; place connotations not explicitly clear from the character string inside symbols [ ]; and highlight literal meanings or explanations using symbols ( ). These symbols, along with examples in context, help the user to grasp quickly various usages.

The dictionary has a *pinyin* index and a radical index with 227 elements. The following appendices are also included: a chronology of Chinese history; a list of weights and measures; a list of chemical elements; a comparative listing of *pinyin* and Cyrillic spellings.

The otherwise excellent *Chinese-Russian Dictionary* has two shortcomings. First, it does not indicate whether a character is used as a surname. Second, unlike most dictionaries using simplified characters, it does not include conversion tables of simplified to traditional or traditional to simplified characters.

HANYU CHENGYU CIDIAN 汉语成语词典

The *Hanyu Chengyu Cidian (A Dictionary of Chinese Idioms)* was compiled by the Chinese Language Department of Gansu Normal University. Published in August, 1978, by the Shanghai Education Press, it represents the most ambitious dictionary of idioms from the PRC to date. It contains approximately fifty-five hundred entries, making it considerably larger than the 1973 *Hanyu Chengyu Xiao-Cidian (A Small Dictionary of Chinese Idioms)* which has approximately three thousand entries. While this is smaller than some dictionaries available from Hong Kong or Taiwan, it is the best and most up-to-date source for dealing with idioms used in PRC publications. In addition, the editors have taken considerable pains to provide the *locus classicus* of the terms included, a procedure which obviously enhances its value as a reference work. The dictionary might have been improved by following the example of the *Hanyu Chengyu Cidian*, published by the Commercial Press in Hong Kong in 1965, which includes illustrative sentences for the majority of its entries.

TRADITIONAL LANGUAGE DICTIONARIES

The compilation of dictionaries to assist the student of classical or premodern Chinese was discussed at meetings with representatives of the Commercial Press, the Beijing Foreign Languages Institute, Nanjing University, and the Shanghai Foreign Languages Institute. Furthermore, the revision of the well-known encyclopedic dictionary *Cihai* was the subject of a major article in the newspaper *Wenhuibao* (April 20) during our visit. The information which follows is drawn from these sources.

Perhaps the most striking impression which emerges from our observations of lexicography in classical Chinese is the fact that it is being done at all, especially in light of the emphasis on language reform. There was a clear implication in our discussions that the State Publishing Bureau *(Chubanju)* is taking appropriate measures to assemble language research tools to insure that scholars in the PRC will have the means to investigate China's traditional civilization. This impression was reinforced by information gained at several universities that the classical language is emphasized or required in the curriculum of Chinese language departments. Also important is the well-publicized intention of China's classical lexicographers that their dictionaries avoid becoming the vehicles for conveying ideology. As Liu Xiaohui, a member of the *Cihai* editorial committee, stated, "An encyclopedic dictionary is like a history. The data on individual persons must be strictly scientific."

CIHAI 辞海

Publication of the *Cihai*, a revision of the 1936 edition expanded in three large volumes, was set for and subsequently accomplished in October, 1979, the thirtieth anniversary of the founding of the People's Republic. We were told that over one thousand persons were employed in speeding the dictionary work toward publication. This massive effort was necessary to make up the time lost in correcting errors introduced during the Gang of Four period. Editorial policies to overcome those influences were adopted. Among those announced by Xia Zhengnong, Chairman of the Editorial Committee, are: first, in all entries when general political concepts arise from the historical facts in the entry, it should be explicitly stated that these concepts are limited to the period under discussion; and, second, judgmental types of adjectives such as "shameless" should be avoided, especially when used exclusively in reference to only one class or group.

An important feature of the new *Cihai* will be the addition of more than fifteen hundred scientific entries representing newly emergent fields of science such as oceanography, computer science, bionics, and satellite meteorology. These plus the more than thirty thousand scientific and technical entries already in the *Cihai* will be classified according to 120 categories. See Appendix 3 for further information on *Cihai*.

CIYUAN 辞源

Other dictionaries designed for readers and researchers in the premodern language which are now in preparation include: the revision of the *Ciyuan*; the revision of the *Xiandai Hanyu Cidian*; the *Gudai Hanyu Xiao Zidian*; and the *Hanyu Da Zidian*. The *Ciyuan*, long a standard research tool for Chinese as well as Western sinologists, first appeared in 1915. At that time it was designed primarily for the student or researcher concerned with character etymologies. Revision of *Ciyuan* began in 1976 and was completed in 1979. It will be published in four volumes by the Commercial Press. Volume one was published on October 1, 1979, and volume two was scheduled for January, 1980. The remaining volumes were to be published by spring, 1980. As in the original edition, it will preserve the same etymological emphasis.

XIANDAI HANYU CIDIAN 現代汉语词典

The *Xiandai Hanyu Cidian* (described in the General Language Dictionaries section) was initiated in 1958. As its name implies, it is primarily for the user of contemporary materials. The dictionary, however, does contain historical and cultural terms. To enable the user to distinguish such terms, the symbol 书 is used to designate a literary term, while ⊠ indicates a rare term.

GUDAI HANYU XIAO ZIDIAN 古代汉语小字典

The *Gudai Hanyu Xiao Zidian (A Small Classical Chinese Dictionary)* is aimed particularly at the needs of the beginning student of premodern texts. It will be published by the Commercial Press and may be available by late 1980. This dictionary will focus on the three thousand most essential single characters used in classical Chinese. Some frequency counts of historical classics such as the *Zuo Zhuan* (左傳) were conducted in order to determine the character selection.

HANYU DA ZIDIAN 汉语大字典

Another dictionary for premodern studies is the *Hanyu Da Zidian (An Encyclopedic Dictionary of Chinese Characters)*. This dictionary is being compiled at numerous universities and research institutes throughout China under the coordination of the State Publishing Bureau *(Chubanju)*. Like the *Kangxi Zidian*, the dictionary will be arranged by radicals and will include approximately sixty thousand characters. One important feature of the dictionary is that it will contain new characters recently unearthed from archeological finds as well as newly coined characters, such as those used for some chemical elements. Because of its unprecedented size, this encyclopedic dictionary will not be available until the late 1980's.

CURRENT DICTIONARY PROJECTS
NEW ENGLISH-CHINESE DICTIONARY

The CETA Delegation met with the Fudan *English-Chinese Dic-*

tionary group on two separate occasions. The Fudan Group published the *New English-Chinese Dictionary* in 1974. The dictionary was well received in the West because of its inclusion of idiomatic expressions and scientific and technical terms, as well as its general word choice.[1] Therefore, we were surprised to learn that the editors considered their work a "failure." In their opinion, the main weakness was the use of stilted or "Beijing Review English" in the examples accompanying each definition. For these and other reasons the Fudan Group, in conjunction with the Shanghai Foreign Languages Institute and the Yiwen Chubanshe (Translation Press), is now thoroughly revising the dictionary. Instead of relying on English-language materials produced in China such as *China Reconstructs* and *Beijing Review*, the Fudan Group is culling entries from recent English dictionaries such as the Oxford dictionaries, *World Book Encyclopedic Dictionary of Modern Language* (2 vol.), *Webster's Collegiate Dictionary* and *Third International Dictionary*, the *New World Dictionary of the American Language*, and *Chambers' Twentieth Century Dictionary*, among others. Examples of usage will be taken from the above sources and from contemporary English books and periodicals.

During our second meeting with the members of the group we visited their offices and saw their lexicographers at work. The sixty-person group occupies at least three rooms at the Shanghai Social Sciences Research Institute. Workers in one room collect general terms, those in another room gather scientific and technical terms, while those in a third work on the definitions. Each word being considered for inclusion is written on an index card or work slip and coded to show the dictionaries in which the word was found. Additional work slips of illustrative examples of the words are then prepared. At present over half a million work slips have been collected. The editors expect that the new dictionary will contain approximately eighty thousand entries—thirty thousand more than the 1974 edition.

We were asked to comment on their work, but after only a short stay could offer no significant advice. One problem discussed was the lack among their group of native English speakers or of anyone who had recently lived abroad. We noticed the word "beachnik" on one of their work slips and commented that the term was outdated and should be so labelled or deleted. When they replied that it had been found in several sources, we suggested that well-informed native speakers could provide information on current usage. They expressed an interest in receiving foreign advice and criticism, but

---

[1]See "China Tells It Like It Is in English Dictionary," Fox Butterfield, *New York Times*, January 23, 1976.

were hesitant to make any concrete arrangements. Nevertheless, they eagerly solicited responses to a pamphlet of sample entries.

AN IDIOM DICTIONARY

Another project underway is a dictionary of Chinese idioms being compiled at the Beijing Foreign Languages Institute. One group of linguists is culling and refining idioms from the Institute's *Chinese-English Dictionary*, while another group is selecting new entries. The dictionary will be arranged by *pinyin*, and will include both literal and figurative meanings. When completed in late 1980, the dictionary will contain five to six thousand entries.

ZHENG YILI'S ENGLISH-CHINESE DICTIONARY 英華大辭典

At the Commercial Press, a revision of Zheng Yili's *English-Chinese Dictionary* is in progress. Zheng's dictionary was used widely in China after 1949, but is now outdated. The revised version will be based on recent English-language dictionaries such as the supplements to the *Oxford English Dictionary*, and will include twenty-five thousand terms. Editors at the Commercial Press expect the dictionary to be published in about two years.

HANYU DA CIDIAN 汉语大词典

The Commercial Press is also involved in the compilation of the *Hanyu Da Cidian (An Encyclopedic Dictionary of the Chinese Language)* which will include approximately 300,000 entries and forty million words. Work on the dictionary is being conducted in the major universities and research centers throughout China and is coordinated by Su Renqiu at the Shanghai Cishu Chubanshe. This massive work is expected to be the most complete Chinese dictionary ever produced but will not be published for at least ten years.[2]

CHINESE ENCYCLOPEDIA 中国百科全书

The final language-related project at the Commercial Press is the *Chinese Encyclopedia*. The *Encyclopedia* will be divided into subject sections and published in separate parts. The astronomy section has been completed, but the publication date is not known.

SCIENTIFIC AND TECHNICAL GLOSSARIES

The general availability of scientific and technical glossaries and handbooks in China demonstrates the serious national commitment to the "four modernizations" and reflects the goals and orientation

---

[2]According to an announcement of October 12, 1979, an editorial committee has now officially been formed and compilation of the dictionary has been accelerated. It is now expected to be completed by 1985. For additional information on the *Hanyu Da Cidian*, see "Lexicography in the People's Republic of China," Viviane Alleton, pp. 69-102, in *Chinese Language Today*, Australian National University, Contemporary Chinese Papers, No. 13, 1978.

outlined in the National Science Conference held in Beijing in March of 1978. The CETA Delegation acquired more than two dozen such reference works (mostly English-Chinese) in a wide variety of fields, including thermal power generation, oil drilling, atomic energy, general agricultural, and agricultural pesticides. In some instances Chinese-English indexes are appended, a practice which makes these works much more valuable as an aid to Westerners interested in Chinese scientific writing. Unfortunately, the majority of these glossaries do not have indexes.

Urgent though the need is for the dissemination of technical information in China, there are two conditions which adversely affect the speed and effectiveness of efforts in this direction. The first is the shortage of paper, which naturally imposes severe limitations on the number of publications. The second is the difficulty of overall direction and management of dictionary building throughout China. Both Lu Shuxiang of the Institute of Linguistics of the Chinese Academy of Sciences and Chen Hanbo of the State Publications Bureau stated that their organizations coordinated lexicographic work throughout China. Nevertheless, it seems that the impetus for dictionary projects may come from researchers or workers on the local level. For example, the CETA Delegation talked with members of the Shanghai Foreign Languages Institute who are engaged in compiling an English-Chinese Dictionary of Audio-Visual Terminology. This work was initiated by the Institute to meet its own particular needs. It reflects terminology dealing with subjects such as closed-circuit television and computerized instruction collected from assorted United States publications and products catalogs. Having determined their needs for such a glossary, the members of the Institute obtained authority from the State Publishing Bureau to proceed with this work, which is expected to be completed in 1980.

By way of a general note, it should be pointed out that technical glossaries and handbooks are perhaps only second to English-language textbooks in popularity in China. There are entire bookstores devoted solely to scientific and technical materials. Also, scientific and technical training is an important part of language training in China. This point was graphically demonstrated when two members of the Delegation were approached by teachers from Guilin Normal University and asked to record selections from an agricultural journal for use in the classroom. The thirst for up-to-date information in China seems genuine and can only serve to draw the Western and Eastern scientific communities closer together.

SCIENTIFIC AND TECHNICAL DICTIONARIES

The following is a list of scientific and technical glossaries purchased on the trip. It represents recent glossaries not in the CETA library, and is arranged in alphabetical order according to subject.

1. 英汉航空流体动力学词汇
   An English-Chinese Aerohydronamics Glossary, Beijing, Science Press. 1976, 250 pp. (12,000 entries, based on M. G. Kotek, *An English-Russian Aerohydronamics Glossary*, 1960).

2. 英汉农药辞典
   An English-Chinese Dictionary of Agricultural Pesticides. Beijing, Petrochemical Industry Press. 1978, 699 pp. (7,000 entries, with English-Latin and Japanese-Latin appendices of common diseases, insects, and plant disorders).

3. 英汉农业科技词典
   An English-Chinese Glossary of Agricultural Terminology. Ed. Tie Ling Agricultural Academy. Beijing. Agricultural Press. 1976, 582 pp. (30,000 entries).

4. 英汉香料技术词汇
   An English-Chinese Aromatics Glossary. Beijing, Science Press. 1978, 172 pp. (8,000 entries).

5. 英汉原子能词典
   An English-Chinese Dictionary of Atomic Energy. Beijing, Atomic Energy Press. 1978, 1045 pp. (30,000 entries, with a list of abbreviations).

6. 英汉生物化学词汇
   An English-Chinese Biochemistry Glossary. Beijing, Science Press. 1978, 146 pp. (8,000 entries, with a list of common abbreviations, common suffixes, and decimal prefixes).

7. 英汉生物物理学词汇
   An English-Chinese Glossary of Biophysics Terminology. Beijing, Science Press. 1978, 125 pp. (7,500 entries, with a list of abbreviations, prefixes, and suffixes).

8. 英汉植物学词汇
   An English-Chinese Glossary of Botanical Terminology. Beijing, Science Press. 1978, 276 pp. (17,000 entries).

9. 英汉化学工词汇补编（表面活物剂部分）
   Supplements to English-Chinese Chemistry and Chemical Engineering Glossary (Surface Active Agents). Beijing, Science Press. 1978, 56 pp. (2,500 entries, with a list of the commercial names of some international surface active agents).

10. 英汉计算技术辞典
    An English-Chinese Computer Science Dictionary. Beijing, People's Post and Telecommunications Press. 1977, 577 pp. (6,000 entries, with a *pinyin* index and a list of abbreviations).

11. 坝工技术词汇
    A Glossary of Dam Building Terminology. Beijing, Science Press. 1973, 679 pp. (5,000 entries in Chinese, French, English, German, Russian, Bulgarian, Spanish, Italian, Polish, Portuguese, Romanian, and Czech. Based on *A Glossary of Dam Building*. International Commission on Large Dams, 1964).

12. 英汉地质学缩写词汇
    An English-Chinese Glossary of Abbreviations in Geology. Beijing, Science Press. 1978, 508 pp. (12,000 entries, with a list of English, Japanese, and Russian geological journals, a list of common geological symbols, and a list of weights and measures).

13. 英汉道路工程词汇 (修行第二版)

An English-Chinese Dictionary of Highway Engineering (Revised Edition).
Ed. Zhao Zukang. Beijing, People's Communications Press. 1978, 1139 pp.
(63,000 entries, with the following lists: Summary of Main Technical Indices
for Highway Design; Standards of Different Technical Grades (in accordance with strength) of Road Building Stones; the International System of
Unit (SI); conversion tables (Length, Area, Volume, and Capacity, Mass,
Force, Pressure, and Volume Rate of Flow); Geological Time Chart, a periodic chart, and a draft list of English-Chinese transliterated sounds).

14. 拉汉脊椎动物名称

A Latin-Chinese Glossary of Invertebrates (Trial Edition). Beijing, Science
Press. 1978, 454 pp. (3,800 entries, with a total stroke index of characters with
pinyin and a Chinese-Latin name list arranged by *pinyin*).

15. 语言学名词 (初稿)

A Glossary of Linguistics Terms (Preliminary Draft), Russian-Chinese/Chi-
nese-Russian. Beijing, Science Press. 1961, 148 pp. (3,000 entries, with a total
stroke index).

16. 英汉木材工业词汇

An English-Chinese Glossary of the Lumber Industry. Beijing, Science Press.
1976, 148 pp. (9,000 entries).

17. 英汉数学词汇

An English-Chinese Mathematics Glossary. Beijing, Science Press. 1978, 252
pp. (16,000 entries, with a name list of famous mathematicians, the Greek
and German alphabets).

18. 英汉医学及生物词素、略语词典

An English-Chinese Glossary of Abbreviations in Medicine and Biology.
Beijing, Science Press. 1978, 389 pp. (10,000 entries, with a section on rudi-
mentary knowledge and a list of abbreviations. Based on Edwin B. Steen's
Dictionary of Abbreviations in Medicine and the Related Sciences).

19. 简明英汉冶金词汇

A Concise English-Chinese Metallurgy Glossary. Shanghai, Shanghai Scien-
entific and Technical Press. 1978, 586 pp. (20,000 entries, with a list of common scientific phrases, a list of common abbreviations and symbols in the
metallurgy industry, a list of chemicals, a list of mathematical and related
symbols, the Greek alphabet, and a list of common prefixes and suffixes).

20. 英汉油矿词典 (增订本)

An English-Chinese Glossary of Oil Drilling Terminology. (Revised Edition).
Beijing, Petroleum Industry Press. 1978, 751 pp. (37,000 entries, with a
geologic time scale, a diagram of prospecting, a diagram of an oil drilling
rig, a list of weights and measures, a periodic chart, and the Greek alphabet).

21. [翻译参考资料] 世界报刊通讯社电台译名手册

[Translation Reference Materials] *A Handbook of Translated Names of
Worldwide Periodicals, News Agencies and Radio Stations*. (Revised Edition).
Ed. Xin Hua. Commercial Press. 1978, 664 pp. (25,000 entries, with a list of
abbreviations of countries, regions, and organizations, and an addendum).

22. 英汉物理学词汇

An English-Chinese Physics Glossary. Beijing, Science Press. 1978, 388 pp.
(20,000 entries).

23. 英汉无线电电子学词汇

An English-Chinese Dictionary of Radioelectronics. Beijing, Science Press.
1568 pp. (80,000 entries, with a list of common abbreviations, selected letters

of the Greek alphabet used in radioelectronics, a list of symbols, a decibel conversion table, an electromagnetic frequency chart, a list of common wave bands, and a list of radioelectronic abbreviations used by the American military).

24. 英汉汽轮机燃气机词汇

An English-Chinese Glossary of Steam and Gas Turbine Engines. Beijing, Shanghai Steam Turbine Engine Research Institute. 1979, 300 pp. (17,000 entries, with a list of abbreviations and a list of important international steam and gas turbine engine manufacturing factories).

25. 汉日英德,俄火力发电专业词汇

A Glossary of Thermal Power Generation in Chinese, Japanese, English, German and Russian. Compiled by the editors of the *Harbin Thermal Power Generation Journal.* Beijing, Machine Industry Press. 1978, 373 pp. (1,800 entries).

26. 英汉真空技术词汇

An English-Chinese Glossary of Vacuum Technology. Beijing, Science Press. 1978, 395 pp. (20,000 entries).

27. 英汉电真空器件词汇

An English-Chinese Glossary of Electrical and Electronic Vacuum Devices. Beijing, Science Press. 1976, 349 pp. (17,000 entries, with a list of common abbreviations, the Greek alphabet, a list of symbols, a list of radioelectric wave bands and decibels, and a periodic chart).

28. 拉汉无脊椎动物名称

Latin-Chinese Vertebrate Names (Fish, Amphibians, and Reptiles). Beijing, Science Press. 1978, (6,000 entries, with Chinese indexes).

29. 水运技术词典

A Dictionary of Water Transport Terminology. Beijing, Science Press. 1978, 243 pp. (1,107 entries, with illustrations, a total stroke index, and an English index).

3 Language Reform and the Teaching of Language

Language reform in China is divided into character simplification, standardization, and phoneticization. It is carried out by the *Wenzi Gaige Weiyuanhui* 文字改革委員会 , often mistranslated as "Language Reform Committee." It is more correctly translated "Writing Reform Committee,"[1] or "Committee for Reforming the Chinese Written Language," because it is primarily concerned with reform of the writing system. It is only incidentally concerned with "promoting the common spoken language as an expedient to foster reform in the written language." This section describes results of discussions with Chinese hosts at many institutions and observations of the CETA Delegation on the topics of simplified characters, *putonghua*, and *pinyin*.

SIMPLIFIED CHARACTERS

Character simplification in China since Liberation (1949) has been a step-by-step process which can be broadly divided into two stages. The first stage began in 1955, when the Committee for Reforming the Chinese Written Langauge created a list of simplified characters and components, using standardized end products from a collection of simplified forms and from certain simplified forms based on the Chinese *wenzi* (character) principles. Popular response at that time was generally positive. Certain objections arose from the literate minority who feared that they would become the new illiterates, and from publication and other industries that would be inconvenienced by a revised script. In 1956, just one year after the draft was announced and used on a trial basis, the State Council officially promulgated 517 simplified characters and components. A further step was taken in 1964, when simplified components were further applied to create simplified characters by analogy (*zongjie* 总结). For example, the simplified radicals 钅 , 饣 , and 纟 replaced the traditional forms of 金 , 食 , and 糸 , respectively. A total of 2,238 characters were simplified. This number represents a majority of the frequently used characters. The application of simplified com-

---

[1]This and other information in this section was made available by members of the "Committee" and others who met with CETA representatives.

ponents, with certain specific exceptions, such as using the traditional form 糸 in 紧 , met with no opposition.

Characters used in most publications confirm the success of the first stage in character simplification. There still seems to be a lack of standardization in popular usage; shop signs and product labels do not consistently use simplified characters.[2] In a few cases, only some of the characters are simplified, and in other cases the complex forms are used throughout. Titles of books are sometimes shown in traditional characters even if the content is in simplified characters. Nonstandardized simplified forms also appear in popular usage. On one billboard in Shanghai announcing offices for rent, four scripts —seal style, complex forms, simplified forms, and *pinyin*—were used in conjunction. In a copy of *Dream of the Red Chamber* published by People's Literature Press in 1973, some characters such as *jing* 經 and *wen* 問 , which had been simplified in the 1964 document, appear in their complex forms. The printing was also vertical rather than the horizontal form. In sum, the first set of simplified characters consolidated in 1964 has been used successfully in official publications and is widely accepted, although some inconsistencies remain in their use.

The second stage of character simplification led to a December, 1977, announcement of a second draft of simplified characters. The list of simplified characters is divided into two sets. The first consists of 248 characters that were considered less tentative and were used on a trial basis in the *People's Daily* for the first half of 1978. The second set consists of a little over six hundred somewhat-tentative forms that were still undergoing study.

Both sets encountered opposition. The first set was withdrawn from use in the *People's Daily*. However, representatives from the Linguistics Research Institute claim that trial use in the *People's Daily* was intended to be only an experiment, and that once the experiment was carried out, its purpose had been served. The resistance to this second stage in the simplification process seems to be much greater than that encountered in the first stage. The objections to the second draft are of two types. The first has to do with the "unpopularity" of certain specific simplified forms that are too foreign to be acceptable. The second type of objection is much more serious. In some circles it is believed that the first stage had already pushed character simplification to its productive limit, and that further simplification would cause too much confusion and create new problems. For example, 圆 was further reduced to 囗 in the second draft, which makes it difficult to distinguish it from 口 in handwritten form. Problems facing further character simplifi-

---

[2]Complex characters appear on beer bottle labels, napkin boxes, etc.

cation are explored in the article "The Development and Standardization of Chinese Characters" by Zhu Chuan.[3] While the Chinese are pressing ahead with character simplification, many in script reform work consider simplified characters to be an intermediate stage, with a phonetic writing system as the ultimate goal. There are also those who hold the view that character simplification makes computer encoding more difficult. As with most blanket statements, this claim is true only for some system designs. For others, it may make encoding easier. For further discussion, see page 39.

PUTONGHUA

The promotion of *putonghua* has two main purposes. One is to facilitate oral communication among peoples of various regions, and the other, considered more important by the Chinese, is to encourage the implementation of a phonetic writing system. From scattered observation in five cities—Beijing, Shanghai, Nanjing, Guilin, and Guangzhou—we concluded that *putonghua*, although spoken with regional accents, is used as a *lingua franca* in cities. There has always been greater population movement in large cities, especially since 1949. In every city visited, we met people who had migrated from other provinces. Recent migrants tend to speak the dialects of their "home" provinces among family and friends, but must use *putonghua* to communicate with their new neighbors. In time, they may also learn the dialect of their present locale. This practice is especially true of the children. While touring the Great Wall near Beijing, the Sun Yat-sen Memorial in Nanjing and other sites, we heard small groups of people, presumably visitors or recent migrants from other provinces, conversing among themselves in their home dialects. On the other hand, a relative of one of the members of the delegation who now lives in Shanghai, but was originally from Guangzhou, had forgotten his native dialect (Cantonese), and now speaks the Shanghai dialect at home and *putonghua* with people from other provinces.

A cavern guide in Guilin, a local Guangxi girl, spoke fairly standard *putonghua*. When introducing the various formations in the cavern, her mispronounced tones—such as substituting the first tone for the fourth tone, as in *zhaoxiang* for 照相 —sometimes gave her away as a local girl. But when she turned to speak with another guide, she expressed herself in the Guangxi dialect, which sounded faster and more facile than her *putonghua*. This kind of bilingualism is acknowledged and quite expected by the Chinese.

[3]Zhu Chuan 朱川 , *Hanzi Fazhan yu Guifan* 汉字发展与规范 ("The Development and Standardization of Chinese Characters"), *Shanghai Shifan Daxue Xuebao, Zhexue Shehui Kexue ban* 上海师范大学报 哲学社会科 学版 , 1978, no 1, pp. 92-102.

In fact, a teacher from the Shanghai Normal University believes that this type of bilingualism may last another hundred years before the spoken languages of China will be unified.

The official policy with regard to dialects is to allow them to coexist with *putonghua*, although it is expected that they will fade out in accordance with the principle of natural selection. In fact, it was claimed that *putonghua* is overtaking the dialects. As mass media becomes more widespread, and if *putonghua* is the primary language used in the broadcasts, it is safe to assume it will gain ground. Meanwhile, a cross-enrichment between *putonghua* and the dialects, primarily in vocabulary, can be expected.

The delegation did not have a chance to investigate the use of *putonghua* by minority (non-Han) peoples of China. In Guilin, we were told that most of the minority peoples have been assimilated and used *putonghua*. However, we did hear local radio programs in the Zhuang language. The present policy is said to be the preservation of the minority peoples' cultures and languages while encouraging them to learn *putonghua*. Cadres sent to minority regions, as well as those sent to other Han provinces, are encouraged to learn the language of those locales. In certain cases, dialects are recognized as a more appropriate medium than *putonghua*, as in local dramatic performances. If one considers examples from other cultures where the overtaking of a minority language over a majority language is attempted, one might infer that Chinese dialects may not disappear for quite some time, perhaps not within a century.

The Chinese we met do not seem concerned about a timetable for the phasing out of dialects, but they do seem concerned about the rate of popularization of *putonghua* as a "public" language for use in schools and work places. However, even in popularizing *putonghua*, Chinese linguists advise flexibility, allowing for special problems present in some dialects and geographic areas. Such linguists follow three guiding principles: 大力提倡 "to promote with great effort," aimed at those who can but don't always speak *putonghua*; 重点推行 "to promote in strategic areas," the strategic areas being educational institutions, communication services, etc.; and 逐步普及 "to popularize step-by-step."

As for propagating *putonghua* in the schools, the Chinese have a five-year plan and an eight-year plan. In August, 1978, the Ministry of Education reiterated Zhou Enlai's statement made twenty years earlier that promoting *putonghua* be taken as a political responsibility. The Ministry of Education's announcement further stated that within five years all language-art courses should be conducted in *putonghua*, and within eight years all other disciplines should follow suit. How this plan will be carried out is not clear. It seems that training teachers would be a first step. The Chinese have reactivated some adult education programs in *putonghua*, which existed in the 1950's, but have lapsed in recent years. Between 1956 and 1960 there was in Beijing an intensive training program called *putonghua yuyin xuexiban* 普通话语音学习班王 (*Putonghua* Pronunciation Training Class) for cadres and teachers. Each session, lasting six months, trained two thousand persons, who returned home and initiated similar courses. Through the joint effort of the Ministry of Education, the Institute of Linguistics, and the Committee for the Reform of the Written Language, a similar program was reactivated in February, 1979, but it is smaller in scale, accommodating approximately three hundred persons each session. The plan is to hold ten sessions over the next five years. Trainees are nominated by their local organizations.

At the elementary level, the textbook *Xiaoxue Yuwen Keben* 小学语文课本 is used. The first lesson in the first volume of this series, *Hanyu Pinyin* 汉语拼音 , written entirely in *pinyin*, is used for four weeks. Thereafter, *pinyin* is used as an aid for learning characters and their pronunciations. In five years of elementary education, children learn three thousand characters.

Discussions on this subject with nonspecialists in China lead to the conclusion that *putonghua*, though spoken with strong accents at times, is already the language of instruction in universities, where the students and faculty are drawn from all parts of the nation, and that *putonghua* is used in primary and secondary schools in the major cities, even though outside of class teachers and students slip back into their native dialects. We witnessed school outings which bore out this impression. The Chinese admit, however, that throughout the countryside dialects reign in the schools.

As students of the Chinese language, we were concerned with standard grammar and pronunciation, particularly the tones, in *putonghua*. The Chinese do not appear to be nearly as concerned about these issues. As for a standard grammar, there seems to be little consensus. The Chinese do not appear to be interested in enforcing a prescriptive grammar, but are more interested in a descriptive one. Ding Shusheng's *Hanyu he Jianghua* 丁树声 , 汉语和讲话 is cited as an authoritative descriptive grammar. The text *Hanyu Zhishi* 汉语知识 produced before the Cultural Revolution is still being used in high schools. Apparently, there exists no standard grammar for the university level at present, and none seems to be projected for the immediate future. It appears that many institutions have independently produced grammars, often entitled *Xiandai Hanyu* 现代汉语 . At Shanghai Normal University, we learned that there are now two major centers for developing standard grammars, one at Zhengzhou 郑州 and one at Lanzhou 兰州 . The latter has received publicity in the *People's Daily* (April 16, 1979) as the national center, and hence may have official sanction. We learned that in Shanghai, the *Shanghai Yuwen Xuehui* 上海语文学会 is also active in a standard grammar project.

PINYIN

In the 1950's, phoneticization of the Chinese script was declared the ultimate goal in script reform. This declaration has been reiterated periodically. However, as time wears on, it appears that the Chinese are less optimistic about how soon this goal can be achieved or whether it can be achieved at all. While most language specialists with whom we met felt that "pinyinization" can and should be implemented, we gained the impression that literate people at large feel that *pinyin* is basically inoperable as a written language. Although some shop signs have *pinyin* in conjunction with characters, literate Chinese pay little attention whatsoever to the *pinyin*. One man on the street stated that a syllable rendered in *pinyin* means nothing to him, but that he can usually guess its meaning when in context.

A linguist at Shanghai Normal University believes that "pinyinization" can be achieved in a relatively short time, given a hospitable environment. He cites examples from Korean, Vietnamese, and Turkish to support his argument. The Korean example is most striking. With government backing, North Korea accomplished phoneticization with relative ease, while South Korea has not been able to accomplish it. The same specialist, citing the similarity between Chinese and English in the number of distinct sounds, reasoned that a phonetic script for Chinese should be as operable as for English. There is published in Shanghai a *Hanyu Pinyin Xiaobao* 汉语拼音小报 which contains several different types of articles—some in characters only, some with *pinyin* side by side with characters, some in which paragraphs are first rendered in *pinyin*, then in characters, and a few small sections in which only *pinyin* is used.

Pinyin is used at present as a supplemental script. In fact, we did not observe a single instance of *pinyin* use independent of characters. However, *pinyin* is the official system of romanization in foreign-language publications. In the wake of the decision in January, 1979, to promulgate *pinyin* romanization, the system attracted international attention. This *pinyin* movement is much less significant domestically than it is internationally. Domestically, the major effect of the January, 1979, proclamation has been in the adoption of standard *pinyin* romanization for proper names which formally had "irregular" foreign translations. Thus "Peking" became "Beijing," "Teng Hsiao-ping" became "Deng Xiaoping," and so on. Even so, some concessions for long-established historical names are made, and the hitherto irregular but widely used renderings are provided in parentheses. This proclamation has resulted in use of *pinyin* by journalistic, library, and other publication facilities in the United States, although it has also caused great concern and confusion, especially in some Western libraries.

The Chinese themselves had begun using *pinyin* in their library filing systems before this latest proclamation. At the Beijing Library the catalog is now organized by *pinyin*. Some hospitals are said to use *pinyin* in their record keeping. Nevertheless, the one directory we had occasion to consult in China—the telephone book—was not arranged in *pinyin*.

Use of *pinyin* to phoneticize the written language poses two major problems. One arises from lack of word division in the Chinese language. In actual practice, Chinese has always been written in single characters so that word units have never been standardized. The application of word division has been quite haphazard. A linguist at the Institute of Linguistics, Beijing, concedes that in at least 15 percent of Chinese words there is no consensus on what syllables link to form words, but he claims that for 85 percent of the vocabulary, there is "spontaneous consensus" on what constitutes a word. The same specialist points out that, even in English, word division can be a problem. But, with the Chinese propensity to conceive of their written language in unitary characters rather than as multisyllable words, the problem is much greater. Also, even if it is true that there is clear consensus on word units for 85 percent of the vocabulary, creating an authoritative list of those words is an enormous task and resolving the remaining 15 percent is even more difficult.

The second problem occurs in syllable division within *pinyin* words. The prescribed principle is to use the apostrophe to separate syllables where there is ambiguity. *Jian* is assumed to be one syllable while *ji'an* is two. When a consonant is in the middle of a word (actually, only *n* and *ng* would be found in such a situation), and it is unclear whether it belongs to the preceding or the following syllable, it is to be assumed that it is the initial letter of the following syllable unless an apostrophe indicates otherwise. *Jinan* is assumed to be *Ji+nan* 济南 while *jin'an* is *Jin+an* 晋安 . By this convention, the CCP's wartime base should be spelled *Yan'an* 延安 (for *Yanan* is assumed to be *Ya+nan*), but this convention is almost never followed. In fact, we did not see in popular usage (mainly shop signs) a single instance of the use of the apostrophe to separate syllables. However, the correct usage of this convention is observed in some official publications, such as provincial atlases, the tour guide for Xi'an 西安 , and the periodical *China Reconstructs*.

As for separation of words in *pinyin*, we observed three conventions. The first is separation by words, as in *Zhonghua Remin Gong-heguo* 中华人民共和国 "People's Republic of China." The second convention is no separation whatsoever, so that an entire phrase is rendered as one string. An example of this convention is a slogan on the wall of a bookstore in Guilin, which reads *weiren-minfuwu* 为人民服务 , "serve the people." It is no wonder that literate Chinese would prefer to read in characters. The third convention is separating each syllable. An example of this is found in the Chinese card catalog in the Beijing Library. This card catalog is arranged alphabetically by *pinyin*. However, some of the cards have only characters and no *pinyin*, although even these are arranged alphabetically by *pinyin*. Of the cards that have *pinyin*—and these constituted the majority—each syllable is romanized separately, so that 人民日报读本 would be romanized as *Ren Min Ri Bao Du Ben*. This system of word division would be suitable for alphabeticization. However, it may not be best for comprehension when used independently of characters.

The application of *pinyin* in shop signs, street signs, and traffic signs varied both within and between the cities of Beijing, Nanjing, Shanghai, Guilin, and Guangzhou. In Beijing, some shop signs were in characters only while others included *pinyin* in monosyllabic style as well as in word units. The same was true of the other cities, except that in Shanghai, almost all signs with *pinyin* used word divisions and, in Shanghai and Nanjing, a few shop signs were seen in "cursive" *pinyin* with seven or eight syllables joined without word spacing. All street signs observed in Shanghai included characters and *pinyin* in word groupings but without tones. Bus-stop and traffic signs were characters only, but bus-stop signs included arabic numerals.

We did not observe the use of tone indicators in either popular or official use. Without tone indicators, *pinyin* used independently of characters is a difficult medium for communication, especially in applications such as place, street, and building names.

It is reported that some Chinese do not read characters but do read *pinyin*. However, almost all the official people met, from guides to language specialists, have great difficulty using *pinyin*, even for the spelling of their names. University students acknowledged that they had studied *pinyin* in first and second grades but that they had practically forgotten it. Obviously, much political and practical education must be done before *pinyin* can become a medium for communication in China.

It is unclear whether the Chinese have ever explored the possibility of an orthography like Japanese which combines phonetic symbols with characters. When we raised this question, it was glossed over by our Chinese hosts.

In all the efforts to reform the language, the role played by government policy and support is recognized. Before the Cultural Revolution, and especially in the late 1950's, progress had been made in language reform. During the Cultural Revolution not only did language reform stagnate, it even slipped back in some cases. In meetings at almost every institution, the hosts spoke of the need to repair the damages caused by the Cultural Revolution and the need to push ahead from the "stopping point" before the Cultural Revolution. A spokesman from Shanghai Normal University used the phrase *zhengzhi tiaojian fangzai diyiwei* 政治条件放在第一位 "political conditions occupying a central place," in emphasizing this point.

NEW VOCABULARY

Since 1949 much new vocabulary has arisen in China reflecting the new political and social situation. Many of the new terms are actually old terms with new meanings, like new wine in old bottles. Some terms are entirely new, while others such as terms of address have drastically altered. The term *tongzhi*, "comrade," is widely used among fellow students, colleagues, and even by restaurant patrons in addressing waiters. Terminology for addressing professional women remains confusing, however. Among the Chinese themselves, *tongzhi* is often used, but this term cannot be applied to foreign or overseas Chinese professional women. The term *xiansheng*, which can be used for male foreign professionals, would be inappropriate for females, as would *xiaojie* and *taitai*.

Due to the changes in vocabulary that have taken place since 1949, overseas speakers of *putonghua*, including Chinese-language teachers in America, can often be identified by their propensity to use dated vocabulary as *guoyu* (now called *putonghua*).

EDUCATION IN CHINA

China today is undergoing a revival in higher education. The brief blooming and wilting of the Hundred Flowers in the late 1950's has not been erased from people's memories, and the downgrading of intellectual life during the Cultural Revolution is still fresh in their consciousness. Nevertheless, while college education is not available to everyone, the atmosphere in universities is one of optimism. With the exception of certain normal universities which are open to teachers, all other universities are available only to those under twenty-five, which means that any older persons in the twenty-five to thirty-five range, who missed the opportunity for college education during the Cultural Revolution, will most likely never receive a higher degree. Of those who are eligible to take the nationwide college entrance examinations—currently the criterion for college admissions—

only one out of ten candidates succeed. Up until two years ago, university students were drawn primarily from the ranks of workers, peasants, and soldiers. The last class of these students is about to be "graduated." The new breed of college student is by and large intellectual, if not in fact from intellectual family background. However, the universities still remind new students of the three important classes of the Chinese people—the workers, peasants, and soldiers.

EDUCATIONAL OPPORTUNITIES

One immediate goal in universities is to bring their enrollments up to the pre-Cultural Revolution level. The newly reinstated annual college examinations have been administered only twice, so that there are only first- and second-year students by entrance examinations in universities.[4] There may be some politically selected worker, peasant, and soldier students in the third-year classes, left over from the tail end of the Cultural Revolution. Students recruited by entrance examinations follow the new four-year track, while the worker-peasant-soldier students follow the three-year track implemented in the Cultural Revolution. The enrollment this year is roughly three-fourths that of the pre-Cultural Revolution period with the expectation that the pre-Cultural Revolution level will be reached in two years. The faculty size is already near the prior level; or it was never substantially reduced during the Cultural Revolution. The slack in the teaching load at this time is taken up by curriculum formulation. The faculty-to-student ratio is low by American standards, even if one takes into consideration the full student enrollment to be achieved by the fall of 1980. Apparently, part of the faculty is engaged in research with little or no teaching responsibilities.

The status of the teaching profession, especially university professors, has been greatly upgraded in the popular mind. It is considerably upgraded in remuneration as well. The average worker's salary is forty-five RMB per month, while university professors receive salaries in the forty to ninety RMB range.

One observation is that women are underrepresented among university staff, students, and in professional fields. Apparently, it is difficult to combine the roles of mother and career woman in China. Most of the professional women and female college professors we met were either unmarried or have grown children. The only woman faculty member with a small child that we met has sent the child (two years old) to her own mother (the child's grandmother) in the country. Another woman professor we heard about sends her seven-

---

[4]See the *1978 National College Entrance Examination in the People's Republic of China*; Washington, D.C., U.S. Department of Health, Education and Welfare, 1979, 110 p., OE Publication No. 79-19138, for an analysis of the content of the 1978 examination.

year-old daughter to a "week-care" center which boards her child all week (Monday through Saturday).

Perhaps because a college education is rare and because educational opportunities were denied until recently, college students in China seem very serious and determined to make the most of their opportunities. Students preparing for college entrance examinations are perhaps the most hard driven. They are said to study sixteen to eighteen hours a day to prepare for the tests.

Those who succeed in the college entrance examinations tend to be children of urban intellectuals, who managed to receive good educational foundations from their parents in spite of the Cultural Revolution. Younger students (seventeen to twenty) tend to do better than the older youths (twenty to twenty-five) who spent five or more years in the rustication (*xiaxiang* 下乡) program. Even among this latter group some received solid educational foundations at home and were able to continue with their self-education in the countryside. It appears that the honor accorded scholars in traditional China has been partially revived.

Women represent 20 to 30 percent of the overall university enrollment. The percentage is higher in normal schools (40 percent at the Guangxi Normal College), and much lower at technical schools (almost zero at Jiaotong University). Entrance to universities since 1977 has been strictly by examination, so that an official sex bias does not exist.

Expenses for a college education in China are infinitesimal by American but are considerable by Chinese standards. Tuition is generally provided by the state. The most meager room, board, and incidentals cost twenty-five to thirty-five RMB per month or a substantial proportion of an average family's income. Even so, because there is such a premium on a college education, a student who succeeds in gaining college entrance would not be allowed by his family to relinquish the opportunity, no matter how great a financial burden is imposed.

There are two exceptions to the above. First, students at normal universities are supported by the state. In accordance with the tradition well established before 1949, normal university students have their tuition, room, board, and even a modest incidental allowance paid for by the state. Upon completion of their education, they are obliged to take up whatever station the state assigns them, and such could mean the remote desert of Xinjiang or the high plateau of Xizang.[5] In the past, students from a comfortable or wealthy family would not choose a normal university. However, because it is so difficult to enter college now, normal universities get some of the

---

[5]Recently, the state has been said to be taking into consideration individual preference for location.

best-qualified and financially secure students. The second exception is students who have worked for five years or more, who are eligible to receive college expenses and their regular salaries while attending college, but who are expected to return to their work units upon completion of their education. Given the upper age limit on college examinations, few workers with a minimum of five years of work experience are young enough to be eligible for college examinations.

Books are a scarce resource for students preparing for college entrance examinations as well as for college students. There is a severe shortage of paper and printing materials. The present policy is to publish a large number of titles, but in limited quantities. Consequently, many "hot" items are sold out immediately.[6] Library copies are also often scarce. The situation is better for college students who are guaranteed at least their course textbooks. Professors send in textbook requests several months before the beginning of a semester, and the publishers issue the exact number requested. Reference books are available in university libraries, but few students are able to own personal copies of books, including basic dictionaries.

In addition to a student's academic load, each year two weeks are set aside for special training. In one of the four years of college, the student spends two weeks in military training. Another year, two weeks are spent as a laborer. In another year, two weeks are devoted to work among the peasants. Aside from studying, students are encouraged to do exercises. Each day, a period is set aside for free activities. During recess between classes, calisthenic music is broadcast in the school yard, and students are encouraged but not compelled to participate.

Chinese students seem to have excellent study methods and habits. In the early morning (five to seven a.m.) one could see students strolling in courtyards softly reciting their language lessons. Memorization is a method widely practiced by the Chinese. This method comes naturally to the Chinese, who develop this skill and tolerance through childhood.

All students live in dormitories during the week. Only one exception was noted by a member of the CETA Delegation whose cousin with a special health problem attends a university within walking distance of his house and is permitted to commute. Most students in the universities visited are from the same city and go home on weekends (Saturday afternoon to Sunday night) so that the dormitories are practically deserted during that time. The few students who cannot go home on weekends remain on campus and are treated to cultural events such as television and movies.

---

[6]China cannot print books for the foreign market. However, books published in China are often readily available in Hong Kong and the United States, since China sometimes sends printing plates to Hong Kong or the Hong Kong printers photocopy a published version.

While college education is available to only a small fraction of the population, the general population in the major cities seems to have a good basic education and the literacy rate is high. Cab and bus drivers, shopkeepers, and manual laborers encountered seemed to have facility with the written language. In fact, we did not encounter urban illiteracy. Even so, over 80 percent of China's population are peasants who live in the countryside. We had no contact with them and are therefore unable to assess the educational level of the peasant majority.

LANGUAGE AND LITERATURE

The study of Chinese language and literature by the Chinese students is not as favored as the study of foreign languages or science and engineering. Nevertheless, it is an important program in all universities visited. At Fudan University and Shanghai Normal University the curriculum for Chinese language and literature is similar. Language course work includes linguistics, applied linguistics (classical and modern Chinese), and electives (etymology, grammar, etc.). Literature course work includes classical literature, modern literature, contemporary literature, and foreign literature (in Chinese translation). The approach is usually historical and includes literary criticism. At Fudan University, there are courses on specific authors and their works. The contents and texts of many of these courses are being reexamined. For example, at Shanghai Normal University, the classical Chinese course is experimenting with Wang Li's *Gudai Hanyu* 王力 , 古代汉语 , a text once considered overly detailed.

Chinese faculty members were reluctant to discuss the contemporary literature course. Due to the unheavals in the literary scene since 1949, caution on the part of the Chinese in their assessment of authors and works was understandable. It had been only two years since the overthrow of the Gang of Four. Perhaps the Chinese have not yet determined what is safe and correct, and are therefore not ready to make pronouncements. They were less reluctant to discuss the modern literature course. The principal authors included in this course are Lu Xun, Guo Moruo, Ba Jin, Mao Dun, and Cao Yu. Secondary authors include Lao She, Ye Shaojun, Rou Shi, Zhu Ziqing, Bing Xin, and Tian Han. Ding Ling is a notable omission as one would expect.[7] There seem to be no courses in comparative literature at Fudan and Shanghai Normal.

Popular taste in literature leans toward the traditional novels. *Dream of the Red Chamber* is probably still the most popular.

---

[7]In June, 1979, Ding Ling was "rehabilitated." This event had been eagerly anticipated by modern Chinese literature scholars in the United States. It is likely that her writings will be included in the literature curriculum in the future.

While we were in China, the traditional dramas *The White Snake* and *The Western Chamber* seemed to be favorites in Nanjing and Guilin, respectively. Authors of the May Fourth era are also popular. There seemed to be little interest in or knowledge of contemporary literature. Several college students interviewed had not heard of Ai Wu 艾蕪 and none of them had read Hao Ran 浩然, although they knew of him. Their impression of Hao Ran is that he wrote good stories about the peasants and that the peasants probably appreciated that kind of literature. Students also seem to be unaware of the rich literature that has developed in Taiwan in the past twenty years.

THE POPULARITY OF ENGLISH

Since the reopening of China to Americans, and especially since the reestablishment of formal recognition, a craze in learning English has swept across China. Not only is it a favorite subject in schools, but also it is avidly studied by young and old in all walks of life. In some cases, this interest in English has foreseeable practical applications, as in the case of hotel personnel, tour guides, and clerks in stores for foreign guests. Young people are eager to test their English on foreigners on the streets. Upon investigation, it seems that for many the English is self-taught. For example, on a side street in Guilin, we watched a young man drawing a cart piled with about fifteen empty oil drums. He stopped, and when we passed he said something that sounded like "lesto." When we failed to respond, he pulled out a small notebook and pointed to the word "rest." The notebook was assembled with three neat columns—English words, their pronunciation in the international phonetic alphabet, and a Chinese glossary.

There are two well-known institutes in China that specialize in the teaching of foreign languages—the Beijing Foreign Languages Institute and the Shanghai Foreign Languages Institute. The Chinese believe that the one in Beijing is superior. Through an American correspondent, we learned of a third foreign-languages program, at Beijing University, reserved for cadres and government officials. Wang Guangmei 王光梅 (Mme. Liu Shaoqi) was associated with this program in the pre-Cultural Revolution period. She was humiliated by Red Guards in the early days of the Cultural Revolution, but has been "rehabilitated" in the post-Gang of Four era. The teaching of English in other liberal arts colleges also seems to be of high quality. The program at Zhongshan University in Guangzhou is reputed to be excellent although we did not have an opportunity to visit the university.

In most universities, two years of a foreign language is required. The curriculum at foreign-languages institutes is much more concentrated in foreign languages. Students take half of their work in language and the other half in related subjects, including two years of a second foreign language. At Shanghai Foreign Languages Institute second-year English students take twelve hours of classes a week in English, divided into listening, dialogue, intensive reading, extensive reading, and scientific English. They take a total of ten additional hours, two each in linguistics, history, philosophy, Chinese, and physical education. Also, they see movies and television programs in English.

English is by far the most popular foreign language studied in universities. At the Shanghai Foreign Languages Institute, half of the sixteen hundred students are majoring in English with the other half distributed among Japanese (next in popularity to English), French, German, Spanish, Russian, Portuguese, Arabic, Italian, Albanian, and Greek. At Nanjing University, the foreign-language department teaches six languages: English, Japanese, French, German, Spanish, and Russian. Also, there seems to exist in Chinese universities an interest in theoretical linguistics. Both Nanjing and Fudan Universities are interested in establishing linguistics studies.

Currently, the most favored brand of English is American English. A student at the Shanghai Foreign Languages Institute opined that American English is softer and more gentle than British English. Many people study English through English lessons broadcast by Voice of America. Perhaps for historical reasons, the dominant form of English taught in universities is British English. At the Shanghai Foreign Languages Institute we observed a class taught by a woman who had studied with Americans in China before 1949. The material used in her class during our visit was British, and the subject seemed out-of-date.

English instruction seemed to place great stress on intonation, and students attest that they do many intonation drills. Also, the teacher repeatedly exhorted the class to speak with correct intonation. Following the formal class "demonstration" there was a free-for-all conversation session in a crowded, noisy classroom where at least ten conversations were going on simultaneously. The students' comprehension of spoken American English was nearly perfect. Three students from this class, perhaps the best ones, were not present that day because they had been sent to work as translators at the Guangzhou Trade Fair. Graduates from these institutes have high ambitions. Many of them competed in an examination to select translators and interpreters for the United Nations in the summer of 1979. It would not surprise us if some of them were successful.

The calibre of both the English teachers and the students observed is very high. The students are carefully selected and are presumably the very best graduating from high school English classes. Their eagerness and enthusiasm are evident.

Students grasp new vocabulary and idiomatic phrases with ease. Almost all our tour guides had graduated from a foreign languages institute. A favorite pastime during travel was to teach the guides American slang and idioms. One of them frequently used the idioms later in proper context.

Surprisingly, almost none of the English teachers in Chinese universities were trained abroad. In fact, most of them have had no contact with native speakers for many years, but they seem to have retained a high level of competence. It seems remarkable that they were able to do this.

The teaching of English in China is apparently successful but not without its weaknesses. There seems to be some difficulty among the Chinese who otherwise speak good English in rendering large Chinese numbers into English and vice versa. (In fairness, it must be conceded that foreigners who speak Chinese have even a worse problem.) The texts are dated, and do not reflect current English speakers in any part of the world. The audio equipment observed being used in language teaching was poor. The tape played in a second-year class visited at the Shanghai Foreign Languages Institute was difficult for the American visitors to understand. That the students understood the tape was probably due to frequent repetition and interpretation. Compared to the tapes, the Voice of America radio broadcasts must seem infinitely clearer.

TEACHING AND STUDY FOR FOREIGNERS

The only known facility for teaching Chinese to foreigners in China is the Beijing Foreign Languages Institute. However, many other universities have absorbed small numbers of foreign students who require supplemental help with their Chinese. One year at Beijing Languages Institute is considered the minimum preparation for foreigners taking science courses in Chinese universities, and two or three years is minimum for the humanities and social sciences.

At Nanjing University, some tutorial help is available for foreign students. Also at Nanjing University special problems faced by foreigners in learning Chinese are being studied. The staff there recognizes that French speakers have problems different from those of English speakers and so on. Teachers have experimented with new methods of teaching Chinese to foreigners, such as using humming to grasp the tones. In addition, a member of the Chinese Department is interested in developing a set of textbooks for teaching Chinese to foreigners. He recognizes the drawbacks of *Basic Chinese*, the standard text for foreigners produced in China, and seems well aware of texts used in the United States. At the Shanghai Foreign Languages Institute, there is an interest in a contrastive analysis of English and Chinese as a tool in teaching foreign languages to Chinese speakers and vice versa.

Institutions in China seem interested in collaborating with Americans and Chinese-Americans in preparing textbooks and comparative grammars. They are also interested in having Americans teach in their institutions. In the teaching of English, Shanghai Foreign Languages Institute insists that the foreign teachers be bilingual. Some institutions are building living quarters in preparation for scholars and teachers from abroad. Exchange of faculty members and students usually cannot be negotiated directly with the institutions, but, rather, must be arranged through official channels, e.g., the PRC Embassy in Washington. The exception is a formalized exchange relationship between an American institution and a Chinese institution, which may be negotiated through the central government. In such cases, the exchange of individuals within the institutional exchange program can be negotiated directly by the two institutions concerned. In general, individuals in institutions seem reluctant to take the initiative in establishing direct ties with foreign colleagues and institutions.

Almost all universities have expressed an interest in having a limited number of foreign students. As of April, 1979, there were several American graduate students in the Beijing Foreign Languages Institute, a few at Beijing University, and one at Fudan University. Nanjing University also had a few students from European countries. The majority of foreign students in Chinese universities are from Third World countries. These students generally take science and technical courses, while a limited number of students from the West study some aspect of Chinese culture. Foreign students usually take courses especially designed for them, partly because some of them have a language problem and partly because different course contents are deemed appropriate for foreign students. Foreign students may audit regular courses, however.

The living and dining arrangements for foreign students are separate. At both Fudan and Nanjing Universities, foreigners live in separate dormitories. They receive their meals from a separate window in the dining hall and generally eat in their own rooms. Presumably, the housing and meals for foreign students are much better than those for regular Chinese students. Universities generally feel that they need to have special dormitory facilities before they can welcome an exchange of students with foreign countries. At the Shanghai Normal University a dormitory for foreign students is being built in anticipation of a student exchange program. China is expected to exchange five hundred faculty members and students with the United States in the near future. Shanghai Normal University plans to contribute four.

There is a surge in higher education in China today. The universities are being filled with the best talents and brightest minds of the country. Also being considered is the reestablishment of the six-year system in the elementary and secondary schools in order to upgrade education at those levels and better to prepare children for higher education. Some Chinese have raised the question of how China will utilize all these language specialists when they complete their education. A partial answer is that many of them will become guides with the China International Travel Service which must provide guides with competence in every conceivable language. Many no doubt will become translators, lexicographers, and teachers. But the full utilization of all the talent and training in China is a serious issue for the Chinese today.

4 Computer Applications

The present state of computing in China is probably not completely known to any institution in China, let alone a visiting foreign delegation. However, after meetings in Beijing, Nanjing, and Shanghai between computer researchers and the delegation, some light can be shed on ideas and on work in computer processing.

Considering the dislocations of the Cultural Revolution and the uncertainties during the "Gang of Four Period," it is remarkable that any modern computing has been implemented in China. There is no doubt that the hardware lacks large-scale miniaturization. Paper tapes instead of keypunch cards were found as commonly used input media. Magnetic tape, disc, printers, and cathode-ray tube displays were apparently in short supply. Computers were available primarily in research environments. In addition to the low volume of hardware produced, components are manufactured in a cottage-style industry. Thus, quality control is difficult to establish and interchangeability is largely nonexistent. Nevertheless, there does not seem to be lack of research skills, since a few of the most modern concepts have been incorporated in research computers. Rather, there is a lack of sufficient quantity of material and human resources and the modern industrial techniques to use them efficiently.

The research workers with whom we spoke were thoroughly familiar with Western literature. Indeed, knowledge of what is going on in the West seemed to surpass what they knew of activities in their own country.

There was some evidence of use of foreign ideas and basic designs, but, for the most part, everything seemed to be developed from scratch in-house. If a laboratory or university needs a computer, its members either build it themselves or set up a factory to do it. At Shanghai Normal University, we toured a factory employing about four hundred people that made electric metering equipment, tape recorders, and small computers. Computers used in various laboratories at the university were produced by this affiliated factory.

There seems to be little interactive computing in China. Machines we saw were used for batch processing in most places. Usually, a scientist prepares his own program and data on paper tape and takes his turn at the machines.

The majority of programs were written in assembly languages, a Chinese variant of ALGOL called BCY (Bianyi Chengxu Yuyan 编译程序语言 Algorithmic Translation Language). The art of Chinese programming language still seems to be developing. The impression is strong that much of the computing activity is limited to scientific applications, many of them directed at training student programmers.

INFORMATION MANAGEMENT

The first technical meeting of the CETA Delegation in China was with members of the Institute of Scientific and Technical Information of China (ISTIC). It was a wide-ranging discussion covering many aspects of computer processing.

The functions of ISTIC are summarized in Appendix 1. The Institute now has exchange agreements with sixty countries, and collects, collates, and disseminates relevant scientific literature on a nationwide basis. Computers have been used in preparing abstracts and in providing indices to these documents. However, the majority of abstracting and indexing work is still done manually. No foreign commercially available data bases are currently accessible, but China is interested in introducing this type of service in line with the four modernizations.

Storage and retrieval operations are carried out manually with only a few experimental computerized systems at present. However, computer capability is expected, and it was suggested that 1980 would be the likely date for presenting a framework for this type of service. In preparation, the Institute is planning to put up a new building with modern facilities to bring all operations under one roof with some help from international organizations such as UNESCO. At the present time, the staff is engaged in research on methods and other preparatory work, such as thesaurus construction and input techniques. Equipment was described as a major problem. An international market survey of computer products and technology was underway. The final choice of hardware and software will depend on the results of this survey.

Vice Premier and Minister in Charge of the State Scientific and Technology Commission, Fang Yi, recently told the National Science Conference (NSC) in Beijing that, by 1985, China will set up data bases in various disciplines. In order to meet this deadline, the processing of Chinese characters will need to be stepped up. It is quite likely, therefore, in order to meet these objectives, that China will have to implement some foreign systems. China has recently imported a few foreign computers such as a Japanese TK70 computer used to increase information-processing capability at ISTIC. The main problem at present lies in software compatibility and hardware maintenance.

CHINESE CHARACTER PROCESSING

Establishing machine-readable files of Chinese and encoding characters efficiently were matters of primary interest in almost all the institutions we visited. The issues arose at the first meeting with ISTIC. However, there seemed to be no clear policy.

The four-digit Standard Telegraphic Code (STC) is being used for storage of Chinese characters in at least two institutions (Nanjing University and Shanghai Normal University). In the institutes visited in Beijing, the STC was considered inadequate especially in resolution of tonal variations and homophones. Many people were engaged in research in this area, although each had different approaches and was pursuing a different target. We were told that there was no specific program in China to look at the problem of numerical codes for characters, and there was no standardization. However, standardizing internal computer codes for characters is recognized as a desirable feature.

Many Chinese computer scientists tended to prefer the hexadecimal system for internal coding because of its potential capacity. Sixteen bits per Chinese character are used at the present time. We were told that the 16-bit code needs refinement because of: 1. variations in usage; 2. different applications; 3. numbers of disciplines involved. The main goal is to select an optimal code as the standard.

In 1978, a conference on Chinese character encoding was held. At this meeting, four approaches to the problem of character input were discussed: 1. whole character, or large keyboard; 2. component structure (form); 3. *pinyin* (sound); and 4. *pinyin* with component descriptors. We observed research on some of these methods, but there was no evidence that a single approach had been directed. Whether by a laissez-faire policy or because of difficulties in coordinating dispersed institutions, each was pursuing different approaches to be applied in its own work.

The "whole-character" method of input is being employed at ISTIC using a modified Japanese T4100 with a large keyboard and electrostatic Chinese input/output machine. There are 345 keys, each of which represents twelve Chinese characters. The choice of a particular character is made by using a set of twelve shift keys. Each character pattern is stored in a 32x32 dot matrix. Text prepared on the T4100 can be output on magnetic tape for processing on the TK70 computer in the Institute. The results of this processing are then written on magnetic tape and transferred back to the output unit of the T4100 for printing.

At the Institute of Computer Technology, Chinese Academy of Sciences, Beijing, a very interesting project on Chinese-text input was demonstrated. It was one of the very few examples of interactive computing. It used a terminal with cathode-ray display and a light pen. The terminal also had a standard keyboard which is not yet integrated into the system. The system principle for character identification is based on a two-corner stroke code similar to the one employed by the Sinowriter and the system of classification devised by Dr. Lin Yutang. When these two strokes are selected the system displays all characters which have the same code, and a light pen can be used to input the character. The cathode-ray tube (CRT) screen is divided into three windows. The first (top) window contains the text being composed and occupies more than half the area. Below this is a second (middle) window which is used for several functions. It displays sets of characters that are: 1) the thirty-two highest-frequency characters in the system; 2) a family of characters that fits the code entered; or 3) a conditional set of thirty-two characters with the highest probabilities of being the next character to be entered. The third (bottom) window displays the stroke components which are used to identify a family of characters for input. The two-corner code describes the upper (beginning) part and the lower (ending) part of a character. A set of twenty components is used to describe the beginning part of a character. Four punctuation symbols are displayed with the twenty beginning components. A set of twenty-one components is used to describe the ending part of a character. Three of the ending components are duplicated so that window three always contains twenty-four symbols whether the beginning or ending set of components is being displayed.

At any time, if the next character to be input is already on the screen, in any window, it is sufficient to point at the character with the light pen to input it.

The principal sequence of steps and the information displayed occurs as follows. In the *initial* CRT display, window one is empty. Window two contains the thirty-two highest-frequency characters, and window three contains the beginning components. If the character to be input is among the high-frequency characters displayed in window two, the operator points at the character and it will appear in window one. However, if it is not among the high-frequency characters displayed, the operator uses the light pen to point at the component in window three that describes the beginning part of the character to be input. Window three then changes to display a set of components for describing the ending part, and the operator selects the appropriate one for the character being input. Window two changes to display the family of characters that fit the two components selected. The light pen is pointed at the character to enter it. At the same time, window two changes to display a conditional set of thirty-two characters associated with the last character input.

The unique feature of using conditional probabilities to display thirty-two characters most likely to be associated with the last character input will substantially reduce the occasions on which it is necessary to select characters by components. Therefore, it greatly increases the rate of input. As described with the three thousand characters currently in the system, an experienced operator is said to be able to input at approximately forty characters per minute.

The average number of steps per character is between one and a half and two and a half, depending on the subject of the text and the accuracy of the estimates of conditional probabilities. We were told that manual analysis of two and one-half million characters of text led to identification of the thirty-two highest-frequency characters in the complete set. However, at this time the conditional probabilities for a thirty-two character group for *each* of the three thousand characters in the system are founded on intuition since computed probabilities are not yet available. Nevertheless, this probability feature cannot help but improve the rate of input and can rapidly develop better measures of the character-sequence probabilities as text is processed. The system is now under development and, as far as could be determined, has not yet been applied. Part of the problem is that the computer does not have the storage required for a larger inventory of characters.

The researchers who demonstrated and explained the input by structural components mentioned companion research on input by *pinyin* and other character components. They were not able to arrange a demonstration of the research; however, they did describe the concepts.

The research is taking two approaches, although each is based on the use of a four-position alpha-numeric descriptor for each Chinese character. The first approach consists of a four-position code in which: 1. The first two positions of the code are the first two letters of the *pinyin* for the character; 2. The third position is the tone number; 3. The fourth position is a code for the semantic element of the characters. The second approach uses a code in which: 1. The first two positions are, again, the first two letters of the *pinyin* for the characters; and 2. The last two positions are two letters representing the semantic element of the character.

While the researchers were not able to describe further details, we did discuss the human skills required by these two approaches. Their research experience was said to affirm that speakers of Chinese can use the correct tone and still not be conscious of the numerical value for the tone. Also, speakers can become careless with tones and still be understood in context. Thus, the second approach appears to have the greater promise.

Another Chinese character input system we were told about is one invented by Zhi Bingyi, Chief Engineer of the Shanghai Institute of Electrical Engineering. We met with Zhi in Beijing and with some of his colleagues in Shanghai. Zhi's system uses a special piece of terminal equipment which we were not able to see because it was dismantled for a move elsewhere to demonstrate its functions. The operator analyzes each Chinese character into its components by a set of rules based on character structure. The component may be simple (few strokes) or complex (many strokes). The operator encodes the Chinese character using the first letter of the *pinyin* pronunciation associated with each component. Each component is a character in its own right or "linked" to a character. This association of components with natural characters is a valuable mnemonic aid for assigning letter codes to the components once the operator has successfully learned to apply the rules for analysis.

Each Chinese character receives a code consisting of four letters. A simple character that cannot be divided into other characters in the prescribed manner is represented by four repetitions of the initial letter of the *pinyin* for its component. In general, characters with four strokes or less are not decomposed. If a character has more than four components, the rule is to collect initial simple components and to use the *pinyin* of the resulting complex component for the first letter of the code. More specifically, a code of the form ABCD for a complex character is interpreted as follows: A—the first component (generally complex); B—the second component; C—the last stroke of the second component; D—the character as a whole. Zhi claims that, for a native Chinese, it takes two hours to learn the system, two weeks to master it, and two months to reach a speed of thirty-two characters per minute.

The Computer Science Department of Nanjing University has proposed a code for each character consisting of its *pinyin* spelling plus an additional element derived from structural properties of the character. What these structural properties will be is still undecided.

Character simplification was said to have a strongly adverse effect on the encoding of Chinese characters for computer processing. However, if we postulate an interactive multistep system in which *pinyin* is used to retrieve a short list of characters from which the operator then chooses, the simplification of Chinese characters would probably have a beneficial influence on the operation of inputing Chinese. Thus, the question of the effect of character simplification on Chinese character encoding depends upon the type of input system envisioned. Emphasis on the negative effects probably reflects the inclination of most researchers to design for batch processing. An interactive system such as the one demonstrated at the Beijing Institute of Computer Technology would be far less rigid in the requirements made on its users.

LANGUAGE RESEARCH

The investment of manpower in lexicographic projects is prodigious by Western standards, and some lip-service was paid to the advantages of applying computers to it. But, as far as we know, nothing of this kind has been done. Interest in library automation was evinced almost everywhere we went, but, once again, there was no evidence of any work in this field, beyond a small project in the Computer Science Department of Nanjing University. Using computing time on a Siemens 773 off campus, personnel have developed programs aimed at cataloging English-language holdings in their library but had only a few hundred entries in the file.

There was widespread interest in the groups we visited in machine translation. Researchers at the Beijing Institute for Computer Technology have a project in this area. The source languages are English, French, and German, and output is in *pinyin*. At present, the system is intended as an aid to human translators of scientific documents. The output consists of parallel listings of foreign and *pinyin* words and phrases, with Chinese characters added by hand before being passed to the translators. The program is still regarded as experimental.

Fudan University has recently established a group for database research which is in the formative stages. The university has initiated formal exchange agreements in this field with the University of California at Berkeley, Purdue University, Toronto University, and the University of Texas in Austin.

HARDWARE AND APPLICATIONS

There was no punch-card equipment attached to Chinese computers we saw. Output was on line printers: 600 l.p.m. models, very similar to the IBM 1403. Most large computers had one or more paper-tape reader/punches and magnetic-tape units attached. We saw only one computer which had disc units (of Chinese manufacture). There were also a few foreign-made tape units.

At the Institute of Computer Technology in Beijing we saw the 013 computer. This machine fills three large rooms. The Central Processing Unit (CPU), a 20m-word magnetic disc unit, and a large engineer's console were in one room. The operator's console, paper-tape units, line printers, and an experimental electrostatic printer (about one thousand lines per minute) were in a second room and eight magnetic-tape units in a third room. The 013 is an emitter-coupled logic (ECL) machine built entirely by hand using small-scale integration. It has a memory of 128K, 48-bit words. Five hundred and twelve words are thin-film memory with a cycle time of 300nsec. There is a 16K ROM (read only memory) with a cycle time of 500nsec. The rest is magnetic core. A single address space covers all three kinds of memory, and the strategy for using the 512 words of fast memory is up to the individual applications programmer. The machine works at an average of two instructions per microsecond. It has two accumulators, sixteen index registers, and a thirteen-stage instruction pipeline. We were told that the mean time between failures of this machine is twenty hours.

Although the 013 was built entirely by hand, it did represent an early experiment in computer-aided design. The model 111 computer built by the Institute in 1970 was used in the layout of the circuit boards for the 013 and continues to be used largely for work of this kind. The 111 is a 300 KIPS (thousand instructions per second) machine with 64K, 48-bit words of memory.

We were told that Fudan University in Shanghai places considerable emphasis on computer science, particularly on the manufacture of integrated circuits. The main computer is the Fudan 719, a 32K, 48-bit, 110 KIPS machine with two 28K drums, two paper-tape readers, and two line printers. The 719 is used mainly for numerical analysis. University personnel claim to have a separate machine exclusively for language research. We were shown a laboratory in which experiments were being conducted in optical character recognition although not for Chinese characters, but for the roman alphabets. The input font acceptable to the device was prepared on a Siemens 560 typewriter and with a red ribbon. The input paper document was placed in an optical device that looked like an electron microscope. The division of work between the various parts was not entirely clear, but it appeared that the computer did simple pattern recognition and identified correctly the letters of the alphabet. The DJS 17 computer used in this project is, in fact, one of an obsolete line of machines, some members of which are nevertheless still in production.

Shanghai Normal University also has a strong program in computer science and, as mentioned, operates its own factory for the production of small computers. The computer science work is done under the auspices of the Mathematics and Physics Department. The factory at Shanghai Normal University produces approximately ten machines per year. We saw a DJS 112, a 117 KIPS machine with 16K, 16-bit words of memory, and several examples of the DJS 130, a larger and somewhat faster version of the same machine. We assumed that workers at the factory were computer science faculty members and students. However, we were told that it is unusual for students to work in the factory while studying at the university, although many of the workers are graduates of the school.

5 Information Services

At present, the growing realization of the need for greater communication to advance the pace of modernization is creating an emphasis on the development of information services. In China, in science and technology, information dissemination relates both to bibliographic data as well as to raw data, and the collection of general-purpose scientific and technical information is considered to be an important function.

The development of information services is a relatively new undertaking in China. The All China Association for Dissemination of Scientific and Technical Knowledge was established in 1950 to help disseminate current information and increase communication among scientists. Six years later, the Institute of Scientific and Technical Information was founded to act as a clearinghouse for scientific information and serve user needs on a nationwide basis. It had also, as a side role, the responsibility for supplying items of technical equipment. Both organizations came under the Chinese Academy of Sciences (CAS) which, in turn, answered directly to the State Council. The Chinese Academy of Sciences itself was formed out of a merger of the Academica Sinica and the Beijing Academy of Sciences. The main original tasks of the CAS were stated as follows: to define the direction of scientific research; to administer programs; to recruit and train workers; to reorganize and consolidate programs; and to engage in dissemination research.

The major source of dissemination of foreign literature has been the Institute of Scientific and Technical Information, recently renamed the Institute of Scientific and Technical Information of China (ISTIC). Initially, its role seemed to be to act chiefly in collaboration with Guozi Shudian (China Publications Centre) to acquire and distribute foreign literature within China, but individual societies and associations also maintain an independent information function, e.g., the Agricultural Association of China disseminates agricultural information. Prior to 1960 and the Sino-Soviet split, this function was largely aimed at exchanges with Soviet scientific institutions and bulk purchases through bookstores in Hong Kong and Tokyo. The Institute began with a small staff of about two hundred persons, some of whom were engaged in documentation of foreign literature. In 1960 it opened a branch office in Chongqing. In 1955 it founded a current-awareness journal, *Kexue Xinwen (Science*

News). In 1961, an index to Chinese scientific periodicals was issued in twenty-eight monthly parts covering seven thousand scientific serial publications in several languages, rather like *Referativny Zhurnal* in the U.S.S.R. In 1962, the *Annotated List of Scientific and Technical Periodicals* was issued, which contained fifteen abstracting journals covering different branches of science. A large proportion of the abstracts were translations from *Referativny Zhurnal* or extracts from *Chemical Abstracts*, Commonwealth Agricultural Bureaux U.K. (CAB) journals, and similar sources. In fact, English-language sources were most numerous. Translations were handled in the Translation Bureau and involved a great deal of work. During the early period of ISTIC (1956-1966), over fifty thousand foreign texts were said to have been translated. The large amount of Russian translations has declined steadily since 1960. Up to that date approximately 50 percent of all texts translated were Russian. By 1970, the amount was said to be negligible, a mere 2 percent. ISTIC also acts as a publisher of scientific texts, which account for the largest share of published material in China at present. Scientific bookshops are popular and always full. Scientific and technical texts are said to account for 63 percent of all publications.

In 1966 the Cultural Revolution severely impaired information and documentation. Publication of scientific and scholarly journals was brought to a halt, and only political texts of a crude informative nature were permitted. At this time, most Chinese scholarly journals sent abroad on exchange ceased altogether, and in some cases propaganda texts were substituted. Many foreign libraries faced with such a situation simply gave up sending materials in exchange. Since China relied to a large extent on exchanges, library resources began to stagnate. Nevertheless, China did make purchases of certain books and reference tools. For instance, CAB journals continued to be taken regularly by Guozi Shudian for the period from 1966 to the present. There was some disruption at ISTIC and within the CAS structure which impaired the work of documentation. And it is evident that abstracting and indexing slowed or was severely curtailed as a result of the May 7th Movement and dispersal to the countryside. Foreign literature was viewed with suspicion, and indigenous knowledge received a new emphasis. Production of the indexes became erratic, and distribution ceased for a while.

The international interests of ISTIC are now considerable. (See description in Appendix 1, Institutions and Meetings.) ISTIC receives hard copies of foreign data bases, e.g., *Chemical Abstracts*, *Agrindex*, but is not contemplating running foreign data bases at the present time because of technical difficulties. However, China is studying the possibility of introducing such services in the future. *Chemical Abstracts* has received its first order for computer-readable information files from China. The Chinese Society for Chemical

Industry in Beijing requested, and has been granted, licences to use five *Chemical Abstracts* computer files. The licences were arranged through the China National Publication Import Corporation of Beijing.[1] There is an apparent need in China for the transfer of large quantities of scientific information. Translation of foreign text is inadequate to the task, and the Chinese appear to be aware of the danger of poor quality in massive translation attempts. They seem to have chosen the dual approach of translation of foreign text and the selection of one foreign language (English) for the information transfer. This practice is reflected in the large investment in foreign-language teaching, especially English. The present intensity of English-language learning is without precedent, and it is not uncommon to find laborers, peasants, and artisans assiduously learning English.

At present, information storage and retrieval is by manual methods. English-language material now makes up about 70 percent of the foreign-language material. Both Chinese and English materials are handled separately because of the translation problem. A dual service operates because a large number of scientists read English. ISTIC is, therefore, interested in developing a separate computer system for its English-language materials. As computer capability is developed over the next few years, staff members hope to be able to operate in selected subject areas. In this respect, we were told, it is hoped that ISTIC staff will be able to go abroad to foreign information-analysis centers to study modern documentation techniques.

Research into methodology is currently very important. We were told that Vice-Premier and Minister-in-Charge of the State Scientific and Technology Commission Fang Yi had stated at the recent National Science Conference in Beijing that by 1985 China will set up data banks and information analysis centers for various disciplines. China could join, through UNESCO and Food and Agricultural Organization of the United Nations (FAO), international systems like National Information System (NATIS) and International Information System for Agricultural Science and Technology (AGRIS) that would benefit the development of scientific knowledge in China and help the modernization drive. It was also possible that China would implement some foreign systems, e.g., Machine Readable Cataloging, Library of Congress (MARC). Software compatibility is a major drawback. ISTIC considers the large commercial data bases, e.g., the CAB database, CA Condensates, etc., expensive to lease, own, and operate, and does not see DIALOG as an alternative because, even with the possibility of a satellite linkup, costs will be

---

[1]National Federation of Abstracting and Indexing Services (NFAIS) Newsletter, 1979, 21 (2), p. 6.

a major deterring consideration. International cooperative systems seem to offer the most satisfactory method in the long term.

Other institutions conducting studies into information storage and retrieval are the Chinese Academy of Sciences and the Beijing Institute of Computer Technology (BICT), which is developing a library information system for the CAS library. The Academy is a major library resource in China as well as in the greater Beijing area. In 1959, it had about two million volumes, which had grown from a nucleus of 250,000 under the old pre-1949 Academia Sinica. Presently the main collection consists of nearly five million volumes and nearly twenty-five thousand periodicals.

LIBRARIES

China has an extremely lengthy literary tradition. In this respect, the country must rank as one of the oldest developed nations of the world. Libraries in the modern sense have had a relatively recent history, and the concept of user-oriented libraries in the Western sense still has no real meaning today. The first public libraries were established in 1912. These were largely confined to the large urban centers (Beijing, Nanjing, Shanghai, Wuhan, etc.). In the early 1920's there were about one thousand public libraries in China In 1936 the figure given was 1,502.[2] War and revolution took their toll. In 1949 there were only about half this figure. Currently the number has increased to about two thousand libraries, but of these only about a dozen can be considered of a size suitable for supplying practical, modern services.

The Beijing Library was built in 1910 and was known at that time as the Jingshi (Metropolitan) Library. Its main collection predates this period and can be traced back to the Ming Dynasty. It was designated as the National Library in 1958 as part of a network of other significant public libraries.[3] Its modern collection at this time reached some 1,400,000 volumes, including old imperial manuscripts and important documents. The present library occupies a splendid building of traditional style in the center of Beijing and is currently being renovated and refurbished. Planning and thoughtful work have produced an aesthetic as well as functional building, which can accommodate about three hundred readers in about fifty thousand square feet of space. At the time of our visit, the new scientific and technical periodicals reading room had just been freshly painted and the main reading room was still under repair. The present holdings are estimated to be about ten million volumes, 40 per-

---

[2]*China Yearbook of Education*, 2nd edition, 1937.

[3]Libraries comprising the national library network in China are at Shanghai, Nanjing, Guangzhou, Wuhan, Xian, Tianjin, Chengdu, and Shenyang.

cent of which are in foreign languages. The main foreign collection is in French, Russian, and Japanese.

The library employs about seven hundred persons, some of whom have received training at foreign library schools. The library was closed during the Cultural Revolution, and many of the staff were dispersed to the countryside. No destruction of the collection took place; however, the use of the library was reduced. Certain gifts and exchanges continued, but since the library had little to offer except political tracts, some major libraries abroad discontinued their correspondence with the library. Consequently, there are serious gaps in some subject areas. Long runs of periodicals were interrupted, and the librarian said that obtaining back issues to some serials is a major problem.

The library is technically open to the general public, but there is some restriction[4] as to who actually gets a reader's ticket, a circumstance which means that the actual numbers of users for a city the size of Beijing (four million) is small. This is not the only public library in Beijing, but it is the only public library in the true sense with a general and scientific collection as well as current periodicals offering user services. Neighborhood libraries cannot be considered libraries in the accepted sense elsewhere since holdings are restricted to a few items of popular literature and current newspapers.[5]

The library did not seem to be crowded at the time of our visit, although all available rooms had some readers who appeared to be serious scholars, government officials, or army officers. Apparently, only the higher grades of government workers or higher echelons of the military may actually borrow books, though others may be permitted to use the reference section.

There was insufficient time to inspect the main and Western catalogs closely, which were said to be receiving some two thousand volume titles each month. The English-language section contained approximately three thousand new acquisitions recently cataloged with only a minor backlog, probably because of the large numbers of staff available to record the bibliographic data. Up to the present time, various methods have been employed to catalog documents. The Chinese Academy of Sciences devised a cataloging system for scientific libraries in 1958, and the Ministry of Culture devised a

---

[4]While in Shanghai three members of our group found a small but well-stocked library with what appeared to be a public reading room at the Shanghai Municipal Museum. The current periodicals on display contained a number of specialized journals in several scientific fields, as well as scholarly journals of major universities. However, the librarian in charge quickly asked us to leave, saying that the "library was not open to the public."

[5]Small "independent" street libraries were evident and seemed to be quite popular. It is uncertain if these are operated by private individuals or not, but it appears that all people can exchange or borrow popular novels for a small payment or "deposit."

scheme for neighborhood libraries. Some libraries simply adopted the Universal Decimal Classification (UDC). Recently, efforts have been made to standardize classification schemes. The classification scheme for Chinese materials was a decimal system linked with *pinyin* romanization. Older cards had no *pinyin* and were handwritten Chinese characters. No work was being done on recataloging of the older entries. New cards were printed and had *pinyin* for the main entry with tonal diacriticals (see Figure 1). Separate romanization was given for each character with no word combinations (e.g., *nong ye* not *nongye* for agriculture). This procedure seems to indicate the transitional nature of the main catalog as well as official uncertainty about correct use of *pinyin* for subject entries. There does not seem to be a policy for linking words to reflect the polysyllabic terms of modern Chinese. Sometimes words are linked, sometimes not. This inconsistency is reflected in cataloging of books, in official documents, on shop signs, as well as in personal names. From a user's point of view, the present situation is confusing.

dà qìng rén zhī gē
大 庆 人 之 歌 (小提琴独奏曲·钢琴伴奏) [正谱本]
蒋颂建编曲 张 申、焦 [illegible]配伴奏 人民音乐出版社 1978年9月
13页 16开 0.33元

J647.21 48.9441 L885 〔38〕
1978年10月11日编印 8026·3490 78—4663

Figure 1. Library classification card.

The Beijing Library's main activities were described as providing user services, publishing the union list of periodicals and monthly current national bibliography *(Quanguo Xinshumu)*, responding to inquiries on a national basis, and compiling bibliographies on special topics. A National Union Catalogue of Classical Texts *(Quanguo guji shanben shuzongmu)* is being compiled. The library in Beijing is coordinating this work with other libraries in the network. Basically, each library is producing its own catalog. Once completed, the cards are sent to Beijing. The catalog is planned for publication in 1982-1983.

Nanjing Public Library, which for a time was China's main library when Nanjing was the nation's capital, does not have major resources. The main collection was taken to Taiwan by Chiang Kai-shek's nationalist government in 1949. The present Nanjing Library is being rebuilt as a provincial library but lacks the collection to act as a regional resource. Great reliance for Central China is placed on the Shanghai Library which, together with the Beijing Library, forms the nucleus of the present national library structure. The Shanghai Library, with a total collection of 6.5 million books, is, apart from the Beijing Library, the only library serving national or provincial needs. It was formed as a consortium of four other libraries in 1952 and serves some three thousand readers daily. In addition, it is said to serve the nearly 1,600 neighborhood libraries and 2,700 production brigades.

The national library network fell into decay in the period 1966-1976 and cannot be said to operate at all effectively at the present time. In 1955, a directive issued by the Ministry of Culture required all publishers in China to deposit a copy of their publications with one of the national libraries within three days of publication, but it is not clear if this requirement has been complied with. The system of interlibrary loans is basically operated by Beijing and Shanghai libraries, and the system is restricted to a few government institutions. In any case, the national library network was really set up to rationalize the acquisition and distribution of foreign-language publications in conjunction with Guozi Shudian. A Union Catalog was also attempted but has not materialized and must presumably await library mechanization plans. The overall coordination and planning of the national library network comes under the Council of Scientific Libraries, which has drawn up a list of specialized libraries. Basically, it has drawn lines of demarcation between the so-called public libraries and libraries attached to institutes of the Chinese Academy of Sciences, Chinese Academy of Agricultural and Forestry Sciences (CAAFS), and the Chinese Academy of Medical Sciences (CAMS). The academies have concentrated their efforts on science and technology while other libraries have concentrated on general topics and the social sciences.

The situation is now blurred with the establishment of the new Chinese Academy of Social Sciences (CASS), and at the time of our visit it was not possible to obtain a clear understanding of the present library policy in these matters. For instance, the Beijing and Shanghai libraries have a number of scientific and technical reference materials (*Chemical Abstracts, Agrindex, Science Citation Index, Food Science and Technology Abstracts,* etc.) which are also held at the CAS. The Beijing Library receives all FAO publications. However, the Beijing Library did not appear to have any of the major social science reference tools such as Education Resources Intormation Centre *(ERIC)*, World Agricultural Economics and Rural Sociology Abstracts *(WAERSA)*, *Sociological Abstracts,* or *Economic Abstracts*. The major collection here focused on Soviet and East European abstracting journals such as *Abstracts of Bulgarian Literature*. At the time of our visit to the Beijing Library there were instructions displayed on how to use the Science Citation Index, and scientific journals tended to be most prominent. But several current awareness and abstracting journals were obviously not being used. For instance, *Agrindex* lay on a shelf untouched. This condition probably reflects the current state of exchange.

Library mechanization has not been implemented in China, except for Nanjing University Library where, in April, 1979, a small experimental machine cataloging exercise began using a set of MARC tapes supplied by the Library of Congress. The object of the trial was to adapt MARC format to local hardware. Input is on paper tape to a Siemens 773 computer at another institute. All output is by line printer of the bibliographic record. No card output is possible. The work on hand is restricted to about 400 English-language documents. Cataloging of Chinese books is not being contemplated because of encoding difficulties. We were told library mechanization elsewhere was in the planning stage. The National Library had no definite plans to mechanize in the near future. Such were only being discussed in general and would probably be carried out with a nearby institute, such as ISTIC.

LIBRARY TRAINING

The major library schools at present are at Beijing and Wuhan Universities,[6] and the only one offering a formal three-year program is that of Beijing University. It began a special library course in 1947, offering seventy credits, including Chinese bibliography, as electives to all departments. Graduates or undergraduates could obtain certificates of librarianship on completion of course work, and the program helped provide a steady flow of librarians to much-needed posts in the Beijing area and elsewhere. The program was discontinued in 1949. It resumed again in 1952 under new university leadership and began to provide the only avenue of library training in China. During the Cultural Revolution the course at Wuhan University was discontinued, while the one at Beijing was "deemphasized" and shortened.

---

[6]Several other institutions, such as Southwest Normal College, Chongqing, were said to have courses, but no one was certain. However, some technical colleges and middle schools were said to be offering studies as options in their curricula.

We were told that Beijing University Library School was running the only modern course available at present. Courses in information science and computer technology were being introduced. Nanjing University, Fudan, and Shanghai Normal University, among institutions visited, did not offer library training as part of their curricula. The quality of instruction and technical bias towards cataloging of the Beijing School were cited as among the main causes for few applicants for library training. For instance, China has generally tended to favor subject rather than descriptive cataloging. Readers are expected to find books by browsing instead of by consulting catalog cards.

Library training received a further blow during the Cultural Revolution with the disruption of educational institutions, particularly at Beijing where a great deal of student unrest and Red Guard activity suspended classes for several years. However, the present political climate seems to have revived an interest in librarianship, and training in information science is considered an integral part of the "four modernizations." Most librarians with whom we spoke were extremely conscious of their professional status and lack of knowledge of current developments outside of China. Their main area of interest is in library automation and information retrieval programs, such as MARC, Subject Content Oriented Retrieval for Processing On-Line (SCORPIO), and Dortmund Library Information System (DOBIS). It appears that each major library wants to modernize as rapidly as possible. There are major drawbacks: lack of trained personnel to design and operate modern systems; lack of library resources effectively to operate user-oriented systems; and the division between Chinese and foreign-language publications. However, China is determined to catch up and is accelerating its training program and hopes to train an entirely new group of graduates in librarianship by 1985. Often we found personnel or students co-opted from the unversities mathematics or physics departments to implement library automation. Some are being selected for training at universities abroad. We frequently received inquiries about suitable courses in North America or special libraries at which to receive in-service training. On the whole we got the impression of a cautious staff wherever we visited, but librarians were optimistic about the difficult tasks they will face in order to meet increasing demands on library services under the modernization program.

In summary, there is a good foundation for national institution building, but information resources need to be coordinated and rationalized with more effective functioning at individual levels which can be brought about by the introduction of mechanization and modern management. The planning and development of new services and rationalization of existing ones require first of all access to knowledge, equipment, and training outside of China.

6 Summary

At the time of the delegation visit, China seemed to be in transition from a highly politicized society in which foreign contacts were limited and foreign technical expertise was not greatly valued to one committed to rapid modernization with selective borrowing of foreign technology and expertise in many different fields. The new orientation is epitomized in the campaign of the Four Modernizations—the modernization of agriculture, industry, science and technology, and national defense.

Many aspects of intellectual life in China have experienced a rejuvenation as a result of the new orientation. Linguistics is no exception. Although the full implication of modernization in language matters is not clear, it seems obvious that new applications of computer technology to lexicography and information retrieval will be of great importance to Chinese linguistics, whether in dictionary compilation, translation work, or linguistic analysis. There is in China considerable awareness of these possibilities, and some preliminary experimentation is underway. The Chinese are hard at work in many aspects of language study and, after many years of comparative isolation, seem to welcome contacts with foreign colleagues.

Lexicography in China is currently responding to the increased demand for foreign-language capabilities as a result of the contacts between China and other countries. Many new English-Chinese technical dictionaries are in preparation, especially in fields that are of immediate interest in the current stage of China's economic development. Among general dictionaries being prepared is an English-Chinese dictionary being compiled at Fudan University in Shanghai. In addition, new general language dictionaries such as the *Xiandai Hanyu Cidian*, the *Chinese-English Dictionary*, the *Chinese-Russian Dictionary*, and the *Cihai* are major contributions to the field of Chinese lexicography.

In the field of language reform, the press for reform of the written language with the utilization of simplified characters seems to be in abeyance. A second draft plan of simplified characters was disseminated, but its prospects are uncertain. The reform of the spoken language and acceptance of *putonghua* has been more successful although, for the present, a de facto policy of tolerating bilingualism seems to be in force. It is common for people in different cities to learn *putonghua* and yet retain their local dialects for everyday communication. *Pinyin* romanization seems to be in very limited public use. It is seen occasionally on shop signs in conjunction with characters, but not on street, bus, or traffic signs. Where *pinyin* appears, the practice in regard to word division is inconsistent; sometimes each syllable is separate, sometimes two or more syllables are grouped as words, and sometimes as many as seven or eight syllables are combined without a break.

A college education is once again seen as the road to success, and the competition is intense because only one out of every ten applicants gains admission. The annual college entrance examinations have been reinstated, and students must now compete with one another for the few places available. A new four-year track has been instituted for college students. Textbooks, like all books in China, are scarce. Professors must estimate in advance the number required for a given course, and no more than that number is provided. Teaching foreign-language reading skills to scientific and technical personnel is seen as one way to accelerate the incorporation of modern technology. Among the foreign languages offered to Chinese students, English is the most popular in the universities and at the Foreign Languages Institute in Beijing. Everywhere the delegation went, Chinese encountered in the streets and shops were eager to practice their English on the visitors.

In China, each institution tends to build its own computers according to its own special needs and capabilities. We saw evidence of the skills required for designing computer hardware and software in the institutes and universities we visited, but it seemed that the human and material resources available in this field were far from sufficient to meet China's current needs. In the computers we saw, there was a lack of quality control and the computer hardware manufactured in China was not interchangeable from one machine to another. In regard to applications of computers to language work, a standard machine code for Chinese characters is urgently needed, but no clear policy on such matters has been established. The methods of encoding Chinese characters are not uniform. Each institution uses its own approach. An on-line, interactive input method was observed only at the Computer Institute in Beijing. Machine processing of foreign text is being tested by producing parallel listings of foreign words and Chinese expressions (in *pinyin*) with Chinese characters added by hand. It is used as an aid to human translators of scientific documents in English, French, and German.

Information gathering, analysis, and dissemination is as important in China as elsewhere in the world. There is need to disseminate large quantities of technical information to consumers. At present, information storage and retrieval is a manual process. The Chinese specialists in this field are looking forward to being able to automate the process and to gain access to foreign data bases by satellite communications systems. A number of Chinese libraries which were closed during the Cultural Revolution have been re-opened, but their collections of reference materials contain serious gaps. Many Chinese libraries wish to enter into exchanges with Western libraries in the hope of filling these gaps.

Though the impressions gained during the short visit were based on a limited exposure, it seems that the Chinese will be confronted with many problems in their urgent pursuit of technological development—in language as in other fields. The process is sure to be aided by mutually beneficial contacts with foreign linguists in the years to come.

1 Institutions and Meetings

THE INSTITUTE OF SCIENTIFIC AND TECHNICAL INFORMATION OF CHINA

The Institute of Scientific and Technical Information of China (ISTIC) was established in 1956 under the umbrella of the Academy of Sciences. It is now the principal information-processing center in China under the direction of the State Commission for Science and Technology. Starting with a staff of two hundred in 1956, ISTIC currently has more than one thousand in Beijing. An additional office at Chongqing was established in 1960 and at present has a staff of four hundred. The main objectives of ISTIC are:

1. Collection and organization of domestic and foreign scientific and technological materials. The scope of the collection includes periodicals, journals, conference papers, research reports, patents, standards, retrieval tools, catalogs, movies, and video recordings that pertain to science and technology.

2. Translation, compilation, and reporting. The main form of reporting is the publication of scientific and technical information such as abstracts in book form, tables of contents, and indexes. Second priority is on translation of the latest foreign treatises and materials which are analyzed, consolidated, translated into and published in Chinese. In addition, research publications are provided for administrators and science and technology personnel in appropriate departments.

3. Document service. Documents and materials are provided to readers, using either an open- or a closed-stack method. Document reproduction is made on request, queries are answered by telegram or letter, and title searches are made. In addition, scientific and technical exhibitions and meetings are held frequently for exchange of information on research and other activities.

In order to meet the needs of industrial modernization—agriculture, national defense, and science and technology—research has been conducted in machine retrieval and machine translation. To achieve computer-automated information retrieval and bi-level indexing, a key-word list is being compiled.

ISTIC is headed by a Director and Deputy Director. The Directorate is advised by two principal committees—the ISTIC Study

Committee and the Publication Committee. Seven operational offices report to the Directorate. They are General Services, the Academic Division, the International Division, Office Management (secretarial, clerical), Personnel, Logistics, and Building Construction. Additionally, there are seventeen program offices. It may be of special interest to list these to describe better the ISTIC program. Thirteen are directly program-related: Information Acquisition and Collection, Foreign Documents, Chinese Documents, Patent Information, Standards (Terminology, Coding, Measurement), Specimens and Models (includes inventions and models), Audio-Visual Materials, Research on Information Science, Information Services (in response to inquiries), Domestic Information Exchange, Information Research Methodology, Office of Computing, and Office of Graduate Students. The remaining four offices include: the affiliated Institute for Science and Technology Documentation (a service center which may supply needs of agencies other than ISTIC), the Publishing Company for Science and Technology (may also supply needs of agencies other than ISTIC), the Printing Plant, and the Chongqing Branch Office.

The international interests of ISTIC are considerable. The following were acquisitions reported for 1978:

	Items
Research reports	35,000
Conference proceedings	1400
Scientific and technical journals	7200
Patent descriptions	760,000
Information on standards	28,000
Descriptions of manufactured items (samples equipment, instrumentation, and hardware)	120,000
Service and technology films	203

Total domestic and international collections are as follows:

Journals (domestic and international)	9700
International documents (research reports, conference proceedings, and dissertations)	600,000
Patent descriptions, abstracts	6,000,000+
Materials on standards	300,000
Samples	300,000

Information cataloging operation divides as follows: general catalog, Western-language cards by title, Japanese-language cards by title, Russian-language cards by title, a file on Western organizations with brief descriptions, and Western conference proceedings.

The Committee on Science and Technology compiled and published in 1978 more than ten million items. Reference indexes (i.e., literature searches) in some ninety subject areas totaled over 1,420,-

000 items. Translation services were rendered for 1,880,000 items across fifty subject categories. Research reports for nine subject areas totaled 6,730,000 items.

General documentation services include patents searches, microfilm services, and circulation of journals.

In 1978, ISTIC responded to eleven thousand mail inquiries. Special bibliographies and abstracts were published in selected categories. Translation services (for reimbursement fees) were offered in the following languages: English, Japanese, French, German, Russian, Polish, Czech, Romanian, Swedish, and Italian.

Additionally, ISTIC sponsored conferences and exhibitions in various areas, e.g., laser applications, microbiology, isotope applications, environmental protection, desalination, heavy metals pollution, the control of wild oats, and Chinese-character encoding by computer. In 1978, ISTIC supplied its research constituencies with 3,500,000 research document copies and over 4,400,000 microfilm page copies.

NATIONAL LIBRARY OF BEIJING

The National Library of Beijing was founded in 1910 as the *Jingshi* (Metropolitan) Library. In 1949, its holdings were only 1.4 million volumes, as compared with its present holdings of 9.8 million. Of these, 40 percent are in foreign languages, most in English, followed next by Japanese. The Western Languages Cataloging Section currently receives about two thousand volumes per month. Exchanges of books and related materials have been established with some two thousand libraries and institutions in one hundred different countries.

The library includes a new Scientific and Technical Periodicals Reading Room, which was soon to be opened to the public; and an abstracts and indexes reading room. The Main Reading Room was under repair and was temporarily closed.

There was not time to inspect the main catalog closely; but one catalog was romanized by *pinyin*. The new cards were printed, and had *pinyin* romanization with tone marks for the main entry. There was separate *pinyin* romanization for each character but not for word combinations. Although the older cards had no *pinyin* romanization, they were arranged according to *pinyin* pronunciation.

There was some interest in encoding of Chinese characters. At present, Beijing Library's automation activities are in the planning stage, and no hardware has been acquired.

STATE PUBLICATIONS BUREAU AND
COMMERCIAL PRESS

The meeting with State Publications Bureau and Commercial Press spokesmen offered the opportunity to survey the range of current dictionary projects and of future publications. The problem frequently encountered by foreign institutions in procuring the most recent PRC publications on a continuing basis was also discussed at length. The State Publications Bureau lacks organizational facilities for dealing with procurement matters. For the present, ordering can best be handled through the *Guozi Shudian* and the *Xinhua* Book Store with whom direct contacts can be made. There was also reference to the existence of another organization, *Zhongguo Tushu Goumai Gongsi* (China Books Purchasing Co.), but without details or address.

NANJING UNIVERSITY

Nanjing University was established in 1902. Before October 1, 1949, it was known as Central University. It currently has fourteen departments: Chinese Language, History, Philosophy, Economics, Foreign Languages, Astronomy, Mathematics, Computer Sciences, Physics, Chemistry, Biology, Geology, Geography, and Meteorology. It has a faculty of 1,651, with 83 full professors, 69 associate professors, and a staff of 1,490. In 1978, it had an enrollment of 4,200 students, including about 4,000 undergraduates, 156 postgraduates, and about 40 foreign students.

One-fourth of the faculty is occupied with scientific research. It is not clear whether the remaining faculty are all teaching staff or whether administrative and supporting staff are included. One must also speculate as to the extent to which all may be on a full-time-equivalent status.

Before the Cultural Revolution, Nanjing University had an enrollment of 6,500 undergraduates and 200 postgraduates. Since then, there has been significant decrease. Now the goal is to reach the pre-Cultural Revolution level of 6,500 by 1980 through broadening exchanges with institutions within the country, by developing close ties and exchanges with institutions in foreign countries, and by importing advanced teaching tools from abroad.

There are now four special research institutes and eight research sections. Each faculty member is associated with some research group. The research institutes include: Accoustical Sciences, Chemistry of Complex Compounds, Vulcanology, and Environmental Science. The research sections are: Seaweed Cultivation, Astronomy, Crystallography, Mathematics, European Culture, American Culture, Economics, and Religion.

Not all research programs are fully operational. There are ongoing projects in fertilizer research. Economics research is only in the planning stage. When projects are established they will be concerned with national economic planning. Economics as a department is new, and there are not enough faculty available.

The library has a history of over seventy years. In 1952, it had in its holdings only 400,000 volumes; but now its Chinese- and foreign-language publications amount to over 2.7 million volumes, of which 550,000 are foreign-language books. This year the library has carried out with some success small-scale experimentation in computer retrieval of source materials. It is now gradually setting up a system of computer retrieval of bibliographic information and sources—apparently for foreign-language publications.

In addition, the library and the Library of Congress have established formal exchange relations for general publications. The library has received the first shipment of eleven volumes from the Library of Congress, and has also sent a return shipment. It is hoped that exchanges will be extended to include library automation information, publications, and discs and tapes.

FUDAN UNIVERSITY, SHANGHAI

Fudan University was founded in 1905 and was planning to hold its anniversary celebration at the time of the delegation's visit. The university has thirteen academic departments which are divided among the Sciences and the Liberal Arts. The Sciences include six departments: Mathematics, Chemistry, Biology, Physics, Nuclear Physics, and Computer Sciences. The Liberal Arts division embraces seven departments: Chinese (Language and Literature), Foreign Languages, History, Philosophy, Journalism, Political Economy, and International Politics. In addition, Fudan University boasts five research institutes: Mathematics, Genetics, Modern Physics, Electric Light Sources, and World Economics. In the Liberal Arts there are research programs on Chinese Literature, History, and Geography. An economics program is just taking shape. The total library holding in books is somewhat over 1,650,000.

The faculty at Fudan University numbers over two thousand. There are two hundred and fifty at the professorial level and nine hundred lecturers. The balance was described as young teachers. It was not clear from later discussions whether the professorial level includes the three ranks as they exist in American institutions. It was also unclear whether young teachers were approximately equivalent to teaching assistants and/or student teachers in precollege institutions.

The total student enrollment is 4,100 of whom 3,700 are undergraduates and 400 are postgraduates. There are twenty-six foreign students, including one American. The foreign students take their meals separately and generally have better fare than do the Chinese students. There is some socializing beyond the campus, but this is often dependent on personal interrelationships.

The current practice in Chinese studies at Fudan University is to specialize in either Chinese literature or Chinese language.

Foreign literature is studied in Chinese translation. There is regular cross-listing between the Chinese and Foreign Languages Departments. Literature courses are divided into literary criticism, history of literature, and studies on individual writers and their works. Classical and modern literature are required of literature students. Other areas of specialty are: general linguistics, applied linguistics (classical Chinese, history of Chinese language, and dialects), and electives (etymology and Chinese grammar).

SHANGHAI NORMAL UNIVERSITY

Shanghai Normal University was established in 1951 as the East China Normal University. The university's purpose is to train middle-school teachers, college faculty at the assistant professor level, and some senior researchers. Students are drawn from all parts of China. The length of undergraduate work is now four years. During the Cultural Revolution the baccalaureate program was reduced from five to three years. In addition, a small number of postgraduate students stay for two to three years. The three-year residence is more common. Postgraduates do not always work for specific degrees. As with other academic institutions, students were admitted on the basis of political and class quotas. Entrance examinations have been reinstated with a significant change in the quality of the students.

There are ten academic departments which subsume eighteen specialities. The departments are: Chinese Language (and literature), Foreign Languages, Political Education, Pedagogy, History, Mathematics, Physics, Chemistry, Biology, and Geography. English, French, German, Russian, and Japanese are cited as examples of subdepartmental specialities in the Foreign Languages Department. There are three research institutes and twelve laboratories. It was not entirely clear if these laboratories represent separate programs or are simply assigned space. The university also has affiliated kindergarten, primary, and secondary schools.

The total faculty is said to be 1,100, but it is not clear whether this figure represents faculty only in the sense of teaching and research. There are some indications that administrative and supporting staff are included in the total full-time-equivalent faculty count. Nevertheless, there is clearly a salutary faculty-student ratio. The present 4,200 enrollment was expected to increase to 6,000 in the fall of 1979.

Some four thousand undergraduates and two hundred postgraduates are currently enrolled. Most students live on campus, but there are about one hundred day students (commuters). Tuition, board, and stipends are free to all students. Upon graduation, students, in the spirit of socialist cooperation, are expected to repay their debt to the government by working wherever special needs exist. Oftentimes, students are not assigned to their home or province. The exceptions are graduates from Xizang (Tibet), Xinjiang (Sinkiang), and other relatively underdeveloped areas who are requested to return to their home areas.

There are no foreign students at the university. The principal reason offered was that there are no dormitory facilities to house them. The Chinese feel that foreign students would not accommodate well to Chinese student facilities.[1] Formerly foreign students had been placed with Chinese as roommates. The university is building a dormitory for foreign students.

To date, no Shanghai Normal University students have been sent abroad. Some faculty have been sent to Europe but none to the United States. In the near future four students and faculty will be sent to the United States.

The library at Shanghai Normal has over one million books and related items. Western periodicals and newspapers seemed to be dated. It is one of the institutions with which the Library of Congress has established an exchange program.

A second campus was recently established for students in electronics. It is jointly administered by the university and the Municipal Electronic Meters Bureau of Shanghai. There is also a school-run factory-workshop which serves the institution's educational and scientific research purposes. Finished products include oscilloscopes, computers, and tape recorders. The workers are specifically staffed for such production and are neither students nor university technicians even though the appropriate departments determine the kind of equipment produced. The school also sells equipment to factories, plants, and government offices, for which it is fully reimbursed. The university can use such funds for whatever purposes it deems necessary. From time to time, faculty will accommodate research and service requests for outside agencies. No charges are involved if the work does not entail an unusually large amount of time and resources.

INSTITUTE OF COMPUTER TECHNOLOGY

The Institute of Computer Technology (ICT), originally known as The Institute of Computational Techniques, was established at the Chinese Academy of Sciences in 1956. A number of other computer design and development institutes were also established in Shanghai, Shenyang, Jinan, and Chengdu. However, the ICT in Beijing is considered a leading center of hardware development, and in 1958 built China's first digital computer.

---

[1]There were a number of incidents in Shanghai during the fall of 1979 between Chinese and foreign students which seemed to bear out this point.

The ICT has active research concerns in energy studies, computer applications to automatic machine tooling, atomic energy, aerodynamics, meteorology, and structure analysis. It is also developing computer-assisted instruction systems, information retrieval programs, and the application of the APL language for interactive problem solving. ICT in Shanghai is also establishing its preeminence in hardware development. The Computer Technology Center of Qinghua University is quite active. It stresses applications of data-processing in factory automation and has developed small computers for numerical control of machine tools. It is quite possible that all of these computer research centers are sometimes confused in identity. The Beijing ICT appears to have a clear connection with the Chinese Academy of Sciences. Some of the other centers (including several not listed here) are at times dually subordinate to the Academy and to local authorities (i.e., municipal or provincial units).

Appendix

2 Meetings

BEIJING

11 APRIL 1979

Institute of Scientific and Technical Information of China (ISTIC) *
中国科学技术情报研究所
Yao Weifan, 姚维范 Director of Information Methodology
Chen Binggang, 陈炳刚 Information Methodology, Meth. Division
Chen Tongbao, 陈通宝 Computer Division
Jiang Yingpeng, 蒋映鹏 Computer Division
Wang Xiaochu, 王晓初 Foreign Affairs Section
Fourteen other participants

12 APRIL

Institute of Linguistics and Philology 语言研究所
(ILP), * Chinese Academy of Social Sciences* 中国社会科学院
 (CASS); State Publications Bureau 国家出版局
(SPB); Commercial Press 商务印书馆 *(CP); Language
Reform Committee* 文字改革委员会 *(LRC)*
Lü Shuxiang, 吕叔湘 Director, ILP
Cao Yusheng, 曹雨生 Vice Chairman, Phonetics Res. Div. (ILP)
Fang Houshu, 方厚枢 Head, 3rd Section (SPB)
Guo Liangfu, 郭良夫 Foreign Lang. Ref. Tools (CP)
Li Rong, 李荣 Deputy Director (ILP)
Lin Lianhe, 林联合 Phonetics Research Section (ILP)
Liu Lianyuan, 刘连元 Phonetics Research Section (ILP)
Liu Qinglong, 刘庆隆 Editor, Dictionary Projects (ILP)
Liu Yongquan, 刘涌泉 Division Director
Shen Jian 申坚 (LRC)
Sun Dexuan, 孙德宣 Vice Chairman, Editorial Board, Dict. Sec. (ILP)
Wang Yongling, 王勇领 Information Specialist (CASS)

---

*Individuals met are listed under their institutional group where feasible. An asterisk designates the host organization for the meetings under each date. At many of the meetings there were additional attendees whose names were not given to us.

Xiong Zhenghui, 熊正辉　Coordinator, Scientific Res. File (ILP) (IPL)
Xu Shirong, 徐世荣　Research Officer (LRC)
Zhou Youguang, 周有光　Research Officer (LRC)
Zhu Puxuan, 朱普暄　Foreign Lang. Ref. Tools (CP)

Beijing Foreign Languages Institute* 北京外语研究所
Lin Xuehong, 林荣洪　Editor, Foreign Lang. Teaching & Research
Liu Shimu 刘世沐
Wang Zuoliang, 王佐良　Professor of English
Ying Manrong 应曼蓉
Zhuang Yichuan 庄译传

Shanghai Electrical Instruments Research Institute
上海电工仪器研究所
Zhi Bingyi, 支秉彝　Deputy Director and Chief Engineer

13 APRIL
Beijing National Library* 北京国立图书馆
Bao Zhenxi, 鲍振西　Deputy Librarian
Tan Xiangjin, 谭祥金　Deputy Librarian
Li Xunda, 李助达　International Exchange Section
Ma Fabi, 马发璧　Documents Section
Qiao Ling, 乔凌　Western Languages Cataloging Section
Shao Changyu, 邵长宇　Electronic Computers Section

Academy of Sciences, Institute of Computing Technology* 中国科学院计算技术研究所
Yang Gangyi, 相刚毅　Director
Chen Shuqing, 陈树清　Deputy Director
Deng Qingxian, 邓清仙　Deputy Director
Li Runzhai, 李润斋　Deputy Director
Chen Shengfan, 陈胜凡　Research Worker, 9th Research Dept.
Chen Tongyin, 陈同印　Deputy Director, 6th Research Dept.
Cheng Hu, 程虎　Research Worker, 9th Research Dept.
Geng Lida, 耿立大　Research Worker, 3rd Research Dept.
Li Guanghua, 李光华　Staff Member, Science & Technology Dept.
Li Xiaobo, 李小泊　Postgraduate
Ni Guangnan, 倪光南　Research Worker, 6th Research Dept.

---

*Individuals met are listed under their institutional group where feasible. An asterisk designates the host organization for the meetings under each date. At many of the meetings there were additional attendees whose names were not given to us.

Wang Nengqin, 王能琴　Research Worker, Library
Zhu Zhiyun, 朱致运　Research Worker, 9th Research Dept.

State Communications Bureau and Commercial Press *
国立出版局　商务印书馆
Chen Hanbo, 陳輯伯　Acting Director, SPB
Meng Chuanliang, 孟传良　Staff Member
Wang Heng, 汪衡　Specialist
Chen Yuan, 陳原　Editor-in-chief, CP

NANJING
15 APRIL
Nanjing University * 南京大学
Language/Lexicography Group
Bian Juefei, 卞覺非　Professor, Chinese Languages Dept.
Chen Jianwen, 陳延文　Library Automation
Liu Chunbao, 刘纯豹　Foreign Languages Dept.
Qiu Zhipu, 邱盾朴　Professor, Chinese Languages Dept.
Xu Weixian, 许继贤　Chinese Languages Dept.
Yue Meiyun, 宋眉云　Foreign Languages Dept.

Computer Group
Guo Ruifeng, 郭瑞枫　Professor, Math Dept.
Li Yongxiang, 李永祥　Professor, Electronic Computers Dept.
Liang Side, 梁嗣德　Professor, Electronic Computers Dept.
Wang Xulong, 王绪龙　Professor, Electronic Computers Dept.
Xu Jinhong, 徐道鸿　Professor, Math Dept.
Xue Shiquan, 薛士权　Library Automation
Yang Keyi, 柏克又　Library Automation
Zhou Songshan, 周松山　Secretary, Office of the President
Zou Zhiren, 邹志仁　Library Automation

SHANGHAI
17 APRIL
Shanghai Foreign Languages Institute * 上海外语研究所
Zhang Zhenbang, 章振邦　Vice Chairman, English Dept.
Chen Deyun 陳德远
Chen Shiyuan 陳士源
Chen Zhongsheng 陳中绳
Gu Baozhu 古宝珠

---

*Individuals met are listed under their institutional group where feasible. An asterisk designates the host organization for the meetings under each date. At many of the meetings there were additional attendees whose names were not given to us.

Gu Bolin 顧柏林
Lin Xiangzhou 林相周
Lü Peiying 呂佩英
Mu Guohao 穆國東
Nie Zhengxiong 聶鱄雄
Pan Xunian 潘壽年
Shi Xing 施行
Wu Dingbai 吳定柏
Yan Yeyun 嚴楠芙
Yang Huizhong 相惠中
Zhang Caoren 張草紉
Zhang Daiyun 張岱云

18 APRIL

*Fudan University** 上海復旦大學

Cheng Yumin, 程雨民   Deputy Dir., Foreign Languages Dept.
Hu Yushu, 胡裕樹   Deputy Dir., Chinese Language Dept.
Lu Gusun, 陸谷孫   Editor, *English-Chinese Dictionary* Project,
   Foreign Languages Dept.
Pan Jinping, 潘錦平   Computer Science Dept.
Tuan Xin, 周新   Computer Science Dept.
Wu Jingxun, 吳經訓   Foreign Languages Dept.
Xu Liejiong, 徐烈炯   Foreign Languages Dept.; Linguist,
   Comp. Science
Xue Shiyi, 薜詩僑   Foreign Languages Dept., Dictionary
   Compilation

19 APRIL

*Shanghai Normal University** 上海師范大學

Liu Funian, 刘佛年   President
Chen Yu, 陳譽   Deputy Librarian
Chen Suining, 陳绥寧   Chinese Languages Dept.
Lu Jingcai, 陸錦栽   Foreign Languages Dept.
Shi Cunzhi, 史存直   Associate Professor, Chinese Lang. Dept.
Wan Jiaruo, 万嘉若   Department of Physics
Wang Weiqiang, 王博強   Office of Scientific Research
Wang Xijing, 王西靖   Math Department
Wang Xuehai, 王學海   Math Department
Xu Guoding, 徐國定   Math Department
Zhang Dongwei, 張東韓   Department of Physics

---

*Individuals met are listed under their institutional group where feasible. An asterisk designates the host organization for the meetings under each date. At many of the meetings there were additional attendees whose names were not given to us.

Shanghai Jiaotong University 上海交通大学

Cai Guolian, 蔡国廉　Electrical Engineering Dept.
Chen Peifang, 陈佩芳　Electrical Engineering Dept.
Li Gongyi, 李公宜　Machines Department
Li Yongfu, 李永福　Office of Political Education
Yang Huizhong, 杨惠中　Foreign Languages Department
Yang Wenyu, 杨文瑜　Electrical Engineering Dept.
Xu Liming, 徐立明　Electrical Engineering Dept.

Instruments and Telecommunications Industries Bureau 仪表电讯工业局
Zhou Shouling 周寿令

Shanghai Institute of Automation 上海电气成套自动化研究所
Qian Feng 钱锋

Shanghai Language Society* 上海语言学会

Chen Da 陈达
Chen Guanglei, 陈光磊　Language Institute, Fudan U.
Chen Huaibo, 陈怀白　Shanghai Educational Publishing House
Fan Keqi, 范可齐　Chinese Language Dept., Shanghai Normal U.
Gu Jiwei, 顾篪炜　Shanghai Institute of Computers
He Hanshan, 何汉山　Shanghai Telephone Bureau
Jin Liuchun, 金留春　Chinese Lang. Section, Foreign Lang. Inst.
Jin Wenming, 金文明　Shanghai Encyclopedia Publishing House
Jin Zuyin, 金祖宣　Shanghai Long March Hospital
Lin Rongli, 林榕立　Shanghai "Xueshu Yuekan" ("Monthly Journal of Learning")
Mao Shizhen, 毛世楨　Chinese Language Dept., Shanghai Normal U.
Pan Youxing, 番友星　Editorial Dept., "Ziran Zazhi" ("Nature Magazine")
Qi Yucun, 戚雨村　Shanghai Foreign Lang. Institute
Sun Kewen, 孙克文　Shanghai Long March Hospital
Sun Zongyang, 孙宗仰　Shanghai School for Teaching Foreign Languages through Electronic Devices
Tian Peiming, 田培明　Foreign Lang. Dept., Shanghai Normal U.
Xie Jiaye, 谢家叶　Linguistics Study Office, Shanghai For. Lang. Inst.

---

*Individuals met are listed under their institutional group where feasible. An asterisk designates the host organization for the meetings under each date. At many of the meetings there were additional attendees whose names were not given to us.

Xu Liebing, 徐烈炳　Foreign Languages Dept., Fudan U.
Yao Linguo, 姚麟国　Chinese Dept., Shanghai Normal U.
Ye Jinglie, 叶景烈　Chinese Dept., Shanghai Normal U.
You Rujie, 游汝杰　Chinese Lang. Dept., Fudan University
Zhang Dechuan, 張德川　Foreign Lang. Dept. Shanghai Normal U.
Zhang Jian, 张坚　Shanghai Foreign Lang. Institute
Zhao Chengchang, 赵承昌　Shanghai Elevator Plant
Zhong Yi, 钟毅　Shanghai Institute of Computers
Zhu Cheng, 朱城　Shanghai Long March Hospital

19 APRIL

*Shanghai Foreign Languages Institute Dictionary Project**

Lu Gusun, 陆谷孙　Editor, *English-Chinese Dictionary*
Forty other participants

Luxingshe (China International Travel Service) 中国国际旅行社

Yue Daiheng, 岳岱衡　Deputy General Manager, Beijing
Zhang Yaomin, 張煜民　Deputy Director, North American Div., Beijing
Rao Benyuan, 饶本源　Head, North American Section, Beijing
Fu Xukun, 傅绪崑　Trip tour guide
Cai Kangmei, 蔡康梅　Staff Member, Beijing
Sun Guofen, 孙国芬　Staff Member, Beijing
Guo Chunsheng, 郭春生　Head, Reception Section, Shanghai
Tao Jian, 陶健　Guide Shanghai
Cui Yan, 崔岩　Guide, Nanjing
Wang Guojian, 王甬　Guide, Guilin
Zhang Nan, 张甬　Guide, Guangzhou

OTHER CONTACTS

Chen Suhua, 陈素华　Guide, Zhou Enlai Memorial Museum, Nanjing
Dai Guozhen, 戴国珍　Guide, Shanghai Museum
Bian Jian, 卞徤　Manager, Shanghai S&T Book Store
Tian Rongzhen, 田蓉珍　Manager, Shanghai S&T Book Store
Wu Zhangfa, 吴章发　In charge of production, Shanghai Carpet Plant
Zhang Yuzhen, 張玉珍　Radio & Electrical Engineering Counter, Shanghai
Zhang Zhisheng, 張枝盛　Shanghai Foreign Language Book Store

---

*Individuals met are listed under their institutional group where feasible. An asterisk designates the host organization for the meetings under each date. At many of the meetings there were additional attendees whose names were not given to us.

3 Cihai

The 1979 *Cihai* is unquestionably the most important traditional and classical language dictionary published since the establishment of the People's Republic. Distributed on October 1, 1979, to celebrate the thirtieth anniversary of the founding of the People's Republic, the *Cihai* is the third Chinese dictionary bearing that title to appear in this century. The original *Cihai* was published in 1936 under the general editorship of Mr. Shu Xincheng 舒新城. It is perhaps the most popular reference work for use with classical Chinese texts and needs no introduction among Western sinologists.

The second *Cihai* appeared in 1965. A revision of the earlier *Cihai*, it was compiled by the *Cihai* Editorial Committee formed in Shanghai in 1959 at the urging of Mr. Shu Xincheng. Eventually scholars from all over China lent their efforts to the revision. After several drafts and the circulation of trial volumes throughout China a final draft was prepared. This was discussed in the light of readers' needs before the final revision was published by the Editorial Committee of the Zhonghua 中华 Bookstore in 1965.

Distribution of the second *Cihai* outside of China has been through the Hong Kong branch of the Zhonghua Bookstore. The 1965 *Cihai* includes 97,000 entries including idioms, biographical sketches, scientific terminology, and historical data. It is indexed by radical, stroke count, and *pinyin* and contains ten appendices. This *Cihai* appears in two volumes comprising 4,301 pages. By 1979, the Editorial Committee of the Zhonghua Bookstore was apologizing for the fact that some of the entries expressed the viewpoints of fifteen years previous.

Work on the 1979 edition of the *Cihai* began in 1972. During the ensuing five years political interference with the editorial work appears to have been a major problem with serious consequences for the quality of the early drafts. The editorial staff was publicly castigated by the Gang of Four. Personages no less than Yao Wenyuan 姚文元 and Zhang Chunqiao 张春桥 leveled attacks at both the project and its staff. The results were especially grave in the historical section where the names of a great number of historical personalities associated with Confucius were removed from the early drafts during the anti-Confucius campaigns of the early

1970's. These names included not only relatives but Confucius' important disciples as well. Many were personalities who figure prominently in the *Analects*. Altogether more than forty names were eliminated. Other entries were rewritten to reflect the contemporary understanding of class struggle and the values of the anti-Confucius campaign. References and examples which cited the *Four Books* or the *Five Classics* as well as other early sources were also removed, presumably because of their association with Confucianism.

A corollary to the removal of information reflecting favorably on Confucius was the removal or replacement of derogatory references to Legalism or the First Emperor. For example, for the phrase *touhui jilian* 头会箕敛 from the *Shiji* 史记 which described the oppressive tax policies of the First Emperor there was substituted a ridiculous phrase from the history of the Sui Dynasty that the "Qin Dynasty was the Son and the Sui Dynasty the Mama."

Not only in political history but in entries dealing with the Chinese literary tradition as well, serious distortions were perpetrated in the name of political propriety. For example, it was forbidden to refer to the works of the great nature poets, Wang Wei 王维 (701-761) and Xie Lingyun 谢灵运 (385-433).

Another field in which the baleful influence of the Gang of Four was manifest was science. Yao Wenyuan is known to have taken a personal interest in this area. Under Yao's principles of "opposing objectivism in lexicography and insisting on complete editorial control," many subjects and individual entries in legal science, social sciences, and psychology were either eliminated or distorted. The natural sciences also came under attack. An example is the teaching on chromosomes in heredity and genetic theory. This was excoriated as the reactionary doctrine of blood relationships which states that "dragons beget dragons" and "phoenixes beget phoenixes." It was arbitrarily asserted that to pursue genetic engineering was to support Hitlerian racism.

Since late 1978 under the general leadership of the Shanghai Party Committee, Mr. Xia Zhengnong, 夏征农 Chief of the Editorial Committee, and his staff have been working frantically to correct these politically motivated distortions in the text. In 1979 more than one thousand personnel were engaged in speeding the *Cihai* toward publication on October 1. Editorial principles quite different from those employed during the Gang of Four Period were adopted. If these are adhered to, they will have a salutary effect upon the final version of the *Cihai*. For example, in preparing historical entries it has been stipulated that if certain political concepts emerge from stated historical conditions, the time periods to which these concepts apply must be specified and limited. The material in each entry is to be full and complete and the language succinct. There will be an objective introduction of important facts followed by a short critique. The facts should speak for themselves. Terms are not to be limited in their use only to refer to one class or group in society. Especially derogatory terms such as shameless or gangster are not to be used as labels for opposition groups. Terms which pass judgment are to be avoided. In considering entries which have multiple meanings or pronunciation, the editors will strive for maximal inclusiveness to serve the research needs of scholars.

The deputy chief editor in charge of biology, Tan Zhaigen, 谭 家桢 summed up the new editorial stance with respect to scientific entries: "Science is the treasure of all mankind; it has no class character and knows no national boundaries." Revisions of previously distorted scientific entries have been extensive. The staff has struggled with the oftentimes conflicting principles of reflecting the present state of science in the world and avoiding excessive and trivial detail. In the scientific areas alone, more than 1,500 entries have been painstakingly added. These deal for the most part with newly developed fields of science, new sciences, the most advanced fields of technology, important new discoveries and new theories and teachings, such as: oceanography, computer science, satellite meteorology, high energy physics, integrated circuits, and bionics. The data and material in existing entries must often be revised in the light of information derived from this new learning. For example, the draft originally asserted that there were more than thirty types of basic particles. This had to be revised to indicate that, including the resonance states, there are more than three hundred types.

Appendix

4 Biographic Information on CETA Delegation

JIM MATHIAS

Jim Mathias is Executive Secretary of CETA (Chinese-English Translation Assistance). He was born in 1926 and educated at the University of Cincinnati and at Boston College. He worked in research companies where he managed projects in Chinese language, behavioral studies, and applied linguistics. As Executive Secretary of CETA since 1971, he is responsible for management of CETA files and resources (personnel, computing, support) for development of CETA Chinese dictionaries, studies of Chinese character frequency distribution, and survey of developments relevant to computer support to translation and computer input/output of Chinese. Two of his published studies are: *A Compilation of Chinese Dictionaries*, by S. Hixson and J. Mathias, Far Eastern Publications, Yale University, 1975, and *Computer-based Chinese-English Dictionary of Current Standard Terms*, 1973, Conference on Computational Linguistics, Pisa, Italy, August, 1973.

THOMAS L. KENNEDY

Thomas Kennedy is Professor of History and Associate Dean, Graduate School, Washington State University. He was born in 1930 and educated at Villanova University, Georgetown University, and Columbia University. His teaching responsibilities include courses in modern Chinese and Japanese history as well as in Chinese language. He has published numerous articles focusing on the late Qing period and has recently (1978) published a book, *The Arms of Kiangnan: Modernization in the Chinese Ordnance Industry 1860-1895*. He has been a contributor to the review of CETA dictionary materials since 1972.

KIERAN P. BROADBENT

Kieran P. Broadbent is a program officer, Information Sciences Division, International Development Research Centre, Ottawa, Canada, where he is responsible for developing and maintaining projects in the Asian region. He was born in 1936 in the United

Kingdom and educated at London, Hong Kong (where he studied Chinese), and Oxford Universities. He has been concerned with Chinese translation and documentation of Chinese and Southeast Asian literature since 1968 when he worked for the Commonwealth Agricultural Bureaux (CAB) in England. He was a senior advisor to the Southeast Asian Regional Center for Graduate Study and Research in Agriculture (SEARCA) in the Philippines 1976-1978. He has published several articles, bibliographies, and monographs on China, but his major contribution recently has been a *Chinese-English Dictionary of China's Rural Economy*, published by CAB in 1978. He has actively participated in CETA since 1973.

VIVIAN LING HSU

Vivian Hsu is Associate Professor of Chinese and Chairman of the East Asian Studies Program at Oberlin College as well as Director of the NDEA East Asian Language and Area Studies Center. She was born in 1944 and educated at Swarthmore College, Washington University, and the University of Michigan, with an emphasis on Chinese language and linguistics. In addition to teaching courses in Chinese, she has also published several articles on Chinese poetry and on the written and spoken language as well as two books: *Readings from the People's Daily* (1976) and *Glimpses of Life in Modern China* (in press). She is currently developing a workbook for first-year Chinese instruction. She has been a volunteer participant in the CETA dictionary project since 1972.

IRVING ANTIN

Irving Antin is Director, Office of Research and Projects at Southern Illinois University at Edwardsville. He was born in 1921 and educated at the University of Wisconsin with an emphasis on economics and East Asian studies, including Chinese language. He has held administrative positions at Marquette University and the University of Wisconsin at Milwaukee, where he was responsible for coordination of large grants, contracts, and proposals. Since 1975 he has been one of the most prolific contributors to the CETA dictionary project, both in reviewing existing material and submitting new material.

MARTIN KAY

Martin Kay is Principal Scientist at Xerox Palo Alto Research Center, Palo Alto, California. Born in London, England, in 1935 and educated at Trinity College, Cambridge University, he was a lecturer in linguistics and computer science at the University of California, Los Angeles, before becoming Chairman of the Department of Information and Computer Science at the University of California, Irvine. He is a computational linguist keenly interested in translation, which he believes to be the best framework within which to study linguistic problems. He has served CETA as a linguistic consultant since 1974.

THOMAS COFFEY

Thomas Coffey is a freelance translator of Chinese and Japanese. He was born in 1946 and educated at Indiana University and Yale University with an emphasis on East Asian studies including Chinese and Japanese languages and literature. He was an assistant cataloger of the Chinese collection at the University of Virginia and an instructor at the National Chengchi University in Taipei for one year. He has been a volunteer contributor to the CETA dictionary project since 1975.

TUZ CHIN TING

T. C. Ting is Associate Professor of Information and Computer Sciences at Georgia Institute of Technology, currently on loan to the National Bureau of Standards. He was born in 1935 and was educated at Washington State University. Prior to his appointment to Georgia Institute of Technology he was Assistant Professor of Computer Science at Virginia Polytechnic Institute from 1969. His publications concentrate on development of computer-assisted instructional systems, as well as automatic Chinese character composition. He has served CETA over the years as an advisor on application of methods of character synthesis for computer input.

ROBERT DUNN

Robert Dunn is a Chinese Area Specialist in the Chinese and Korean Section, Asian Division, Library of Congress. Born in 1915, he was educated at Harvard University. He has over 25 years of service in the federal government, 18 of which have been with the Library. He recently compiled an annotated bibliography on *Chinese-English and English-Chinese Dictionaries in the Library of Congress, 1977*. His contribution to CETA has been as an editor for the CETA dictionary since 1974. He has also helped in coordinating the Library of Congress' computer processing support to COM (Computer Output Microfilm) output of CETA dictionary files.

JAMES D. McHALE

James McHale has been Chief of the China Broadcasting Branch, Voice of America, since 1975. He was born in 1926 and was educated at Boston University and Johns Hopkins University. His two decades of service as a Foreign Service Officer were in Asia, Africa, and Europe with focus on Asia. He is a linguist and author of numerous articles on U.S. foreign policy for specialized journals, including the *Foreign Service Journal*. He has supported Chinese-language editorial services for CETA since 1975.

HENRY LOUIE

Henry Louie began to work on the CETA dictionary project in 1972 and has served on its Language Committee since 1973. He was born in Akron, Ohio, in 1925. He received his primary and high school education in China from 1930 to 1939. He is a graduate of Washington College, Chestertown, Maryland, with a BA degree in economics. He is a translator of Chinese for the United States government. He has provided Chinese-language review services for CETA general dictionary materials since 1976.

THOMAS CREAMER

Thomas Creamer is a Chinese-language specialist on the CETA Secretariat Staff. He was born in 1950 and educated at Bradley University and the University of Virginia, with an emphasis on modern Chinese history. As a member of the CETA staff since 1977, his work is focused on editing the general and technical dictionaries, compiling specialized technical glossaries, and monitoring recent PRC language-reform efforts. At the recent 31st annual meeting of the Association for Asian Studies he presented a paper on the Chinese student movement.

Appendix

 Computer printout of French to Chinese machine translation. First line French. Translation in pinyin on lower line by machine. Translation with tones shown by the numbers 1,2,3, & 4.

86 Champ electromagnetique rayonne par une ouverture circulaire plane dans sa zone proche
Tong1guo4 zai4 sa lin2jin4 ling3yu4 zhong1 de 2 yuan2 ping2-mian4 kong3 de 2 fu2she4 de2 dian4ci2 chang3

87 Ajustement mathematique de parametres ionospheriques
Dian4!2ceng2 can1shu4 de2 shu4xue2 jiaco4zheng4

88 Modes propres des systemes couples appliques au calcul des lignes a meandres microbandes
Xi4tong3 ou3 yu2hui2 wei1bo1duan4 de2 xian4 de2 ji4suan4 de2 ying4yong4 de2 gu4you3 fangishi4

88 Conversion parametrique de frequence infrarouge visible—
Hong2wai4xian4 ke3jian4de pin2lyu4 de2 can1shu4 bian4huan4

89 Etude prospective
Qian2jing3 yan2jiu1

90 Elimination optimale des derives lentes dans les mesures de fluctuations
Zai4 bo1dong1 de2 ce4liang2 de2 man4 piao1yi2 de2 zui4jia1 Xiao1 chu2

91 Affaiblissement terr-satellite geostationnaire a partir de mesur
Be2me2 tou2 ue2 zhai4sheng1chan3 xing4hen2

Computer printout of English to Chinese machine translation. First line English. Translation in pinyin on lower line by machine. Translation with tones shown by the numbers 1,2,3, & 4.

77 A linear self-biased magnetoresistive head
Xian3xieng4de1 zhi4pianizhi3de1 kang3ci2de1 ci2tou2

78 Super-narrow track mr head
Chac3xia2zhai3oe1 dao4 ci2kang3 ci2tou2

79 Batch-fabricated heads from an operational standpoint
Cheng2pi1sheng1chan3de1 yu2 chao1zhuo4de1 jiao3du4 de2 ci2-
tou2

80 Experimental study of the external fringing field on integrated
head
Buneng

81 Design of advanced digital magnetic recording systems
Xian1jin4de1 shu4zi4de1 ci2ji4lu4 xi4tong3 de2 she4ji4

82 Disc file optimization
Pan2 wun2jian4 you1hua4

83 An improved pulse-slimming method for magnetic recording
Gai3jin4de1 mai4chong1ya4zai3 wei4liao3 ci2ji4lu4 de2 fang1fa3